Mothering
from the
Inside

SUNY series in Women, Crime, and Criminology
Meda Chesney-Lind and Russ Immarigeon, editors

# Mothering from the Inside

## Parenting in a Women's Prison

Sandra Enos

State University of New York Press

Published by
State University of New York Press

For information, address the State University of New York Press,
90 State Street, Suite 700, Albany, NY 12207

Marketing by Dana E. Yanulavich • Production by Bernadine Dawes

Excerpts from *How It's Done, 1st edition,* by E. S. Adler and R. Clark. © 1999.
Reprinted with permission of Wadsworth Publishing, a division of Thomson
Learning. Fax 800 730-2215.

Library of Congress Cataloging-in-Publication Data

Enos, Sandra, 1949–
    Mothering from the inside : parenting in a women's prison / Sandra Enos.
    p.  cm. — (SUNY series in women, crime, and criminology)
    Includes bibliographical references and indexes.
    ISBN 0-7914-4849-5 (alk. paper) — ISBN 0-7914-4850-9 (pbk. : alk. paper)
    1. Women prisoners—United States. 2. Absentee mothers—United States.
    3. Motherhood. 4. Children of women prisoners—United States. 5. Prisoners'
    families—United States. I. Title. II. Series.

HV9471.E5 2001
362.7—dc21                                          00-032952

1  2  3  4  5  6  7  8  9  10

# Contents

# Acknowledgments

The birth, nurturing, and development of this project is shared by many mothers and fathers. Members of this book's family include those from the academic and the public service communities, those inmate mothers who participated in this study, and the various colleagues, mentors and others who assisted in the thinking, rethinking, and development of this research.

First of all, special recognition must be paid to my teachers, who are all talented sociologists, and other scholars at the University of Connecticut and my colleagues at Rhode Island College. I returned to graduate work late in life and found that there was no better place for me to learn about doing sociology than UCONN. My teachers there introduced me to qualitative methodology (Robert Broadhead and Clint Sanders), to feminist theorizing and critical analysis (Myra Marx Ferree), to American women's history (Susan Porter Benson), and to social psychology and the diversity of family (Ronald Taylor). Their contributions are evident in this book. Other colleagues and mentors at Rhode Island College and the University of Rhode Island encouraged me to return to graduate school to pursue my doctorate. Emily Stier Adler, Pamela Irving Jackson, and Roger Clark at Rhode Island College have encouraged my teaching and research, and Mary Ellen Reilly, Barbara Luebke, and Jody Brown at the University of Rhode Island could not have been more supportive as friends and advocates of my work.

Roberta Richman, the warden of the Women's Prison in Rhode Island, made this project and many other research projects possible. Her willingness to open up the institution to outsiders, to those who might be critical, has enriched not only the academic world and scholarship about the population of women in prison but has also given women inmates access to some important services. Those in the correctional field and in the local community recognize Ms. Richman as a progressive and enlightened administrator of a well-run institution. She, on the other hand, is modest about her achievements and suggests that, given the nature of correctional institutions, even the best administration can achieve little "good work" behind bars; she is a strong advocate of community-based corrections. Her investment in this research was essential to its completion. Other staff at the Women's Prison were also helpful, not only in guiding me through the various administrative and institutional channels but also in helping me to understand the setting. Special appreciation is extended to Alberta Baccari, coordinator of the parenting program, who provided me entry to the program and assisted in arranging interviews.

In the course of completing this research, I met nearly one hundred inmate mothers and their children in the parenting program. Many patiently tried to help me understand mothering in prison. All twenty-five inmate mothers who participated in this research deserve my special appreciation. I have maintained contact with one inmate mother and for several years now have periodically visited with her in prison. She has become a good friend and helped me enormously as I struggle to "speak the truth" to my students in the courses Crime and Criminal Justice, Law and Society, and Women, Crime, and Justice. She has also made important contributions to this research, to how I think about race and ethnicity, and to how I think about doing research.

Three anonymous reviewers of the manuscript helped me to clarify my analysis and made this a much stronger book. The staff at SUNY Press was enormously helpful, especially to a first-time author of a book. I had wonderful conversations with Nancy Ellegate about matters related to publishing, permissions, and the like and found her to be a glowing beacon in what can be a difficult world for a first-time author to navigate.

Finally, I would like to acknowledge my indebtedness to my own family and friends who have helped me to create and sustain this work. My mother, Lucille, brother John, and sister Marcia have always nurtured me in ways I am only beginning to understand. My network of friends has provided a critical mass of support and love tempered with challenges to my thinking and storytelling. I hope this work deserves the time, attention, and energy of many who have played a part in it.

# Chapter 1

# Mothers in Prison: The Impact of Race and Ethnicity

There is a long tradition in the United States of anxiety about the state of the family (Gordon 1988; Stacey 1990). The disappearance of the family unit, the undermining of traditional "family values," the weakening of family bonds under the onslaught of a changing society, and accompanying concerns about the state of the family are not new issues. Recently, advocates and government officials have promoted public policies that are more family sensitive, that is, that support families. However, despite all the public hand-wringing about maintaining and supporting the family unit, there appears to be little interest on the part of the public or on the part of policy makers about the impact of harsh criminal justice policies on men, women, and their children. The war on crime has been characterized by some as a war on women, the poor, and minorities (Donziger 1996). The impact of the harsh sentencing policies that have a disproportionate effect on women, on the disadvantaged, and on people of color (Raeder 1993) is likely to grow more serious as changes in child-welfare policy and welfare reform also continue to evolve and work their way into local communities. The impact of strict and severe sentencing has meant that increasing numbers of children are affected by the imprisonment of their parents. As has been reported in the popular press, the populations of incarcerated men and women continue their twenty-year climb to unprecedented heights. At midyear 1998, more than 1.8 million men and women were confined in state and federal prisons and jails, accounting for 1 out of every 150 residents (Gilliard 1999). Although in 1996 the United States lost its international lead in per capita imprisonment to Russia and fell to second place, this nation is nonetheless

1

a leader in incarcerating its members, especially compared to Western European countries (Mauer 1997). Nationwide, women account for approximately 6.4 percent of the prison population and approximately 10.8 percent of the population in jail. While the numbers of male prison and jail inmates has increased by 150 percent between 1985 and 1998, the comparable percentage increase for women is 260 percent. Despite the fact that the number of women behind bars has been increasing, the dilemmas presented by larger numbers of imprisoned women echo those identified by those researching the history and development of women's prisons in earlier eras (Rafter 1997). Because women account for a relatively small number in increasingly large correctional enterprises, their needs and issues either are ignored or made to conform to the institutional norms, regulations, and programs designed with dangerous male inmates in mind.

This book examines how women manage motherhood from inside a women's prison. It is the result of participant observation and intensive interviews conducted over a three-year period. A central concern here is understanding how inmate mothers construct motherhood and do mothering while incarcerated. How women manage motherhood while they are incarcerated, how living arrangements for children are determined, and how relationships between mothers and their children are developed and maintained are the foci of this book. Special attention is paid to race and ethnicity and to families as these factors affect women in prison and their children.

In some demographic characteristics, the female population mirrors the male population. Both populations are made up of large numbers of ethnic and racial minorities. Forty-six percent of the females and 45.5 percent of the males are black; 14 percent of the females and 16.8 percent of the males are Hispanic. The median ages for female inmates and male inmates are thirty-one and thirty years, respectively; 62 percent of the women and 66 percent of the men have less than a high school education (Owen and Bloom 1995). However, women inmates differ statistically from male inmates in several areas. A higher percentage of women have members of their family in prison (47 percent of the women versus 37 percent of the men); they are less likely to be serving time for violent offenses (32 percent of females versus 47 percent of males); they are serving shorter sentences (mean of 105 months versus 153 months for men); and they are more likely to be parents (78 percent versus 64 percent) than are their male counter-parts (Snell 1994). Among the critical differences presented by male and female inmates are those that have to do with the importance of family and children. It is estimated that 80 percent of these women are mothers with children, and 66 percent of them have children under the age of eighteen (Bloom and Steinhart 1993). Seventy percent of these women were living with their children before incarceration (Snell 1994). Of the males, only 64 percent are fathers, as mentioned, and about a half of those inmates (53 percent) were living with their children at the time of arrest.

Arranging and managing the care of children of female inmates present incarcerated women and their families with a variety of tasks and burdens. Unlike male inmates, who may be somewhat peripheral to work associated with family caretaking and kinwork (Swan 1981), most female inmates lead lives that are embedded in complex arrange-ments of shared child care, pooled resources, and other strategies to enhance family survival. Their absence from their families often places the family itself in jeopardy.

Many have said about the recent incarceration boom that "we are not winning the war on drugs, but we are taking a lot of prisoners." With the significant increases in the incarcerated population, the num-bers of children who are affected by parental absence have also increased. The Bureau of Justice estimates that nearly 2 million children have parents or relatives who are in prison or in jail (Butterfield 1999). Be-cause of the gendered nature of child care, most children of inmates had been living with their mothers prior to incarceration. Because of this fact, children of male inmates are less likely to suffer disruption in their living arrangements than are those of female inmates. Gen-dered differences in primary child-care responsibilities prior to incar-ceration mean that male inmates are more likely to be able to leave their children with primary care providers—that is, with the mothers of their children. Women, as customary primary caretakers, do not have the option in many instances to leave the children with husbands and partners, and must develop and identify other providers of care (Farrell 1998). These arrangements are sometimes mediated by the involve-ment of the state, in the organizational form of child welfare. In other cases, women and their families struggle to find places for children to live without the involvement of state agencies. In this chapter, I will review the literature on where children of inmate mothers live while the mothers are incarcerated and on how women manage motherhood in prison. Factors related to the selection of places to live for children will also be investigated with special attention to race and ethnicity and to "paths to prison."

## OPTIONS AND PATTERNS OF PLACEMENT

One important aspect of managing motherhood and mothering during incarceration involves the determination of living arrangements for children. Using a formula devised by Johnston (1995c), we can estimate that having 145,000 women in jails and prisons results in more than 230,000 children living apart from their mothers. Where children live during the incarceration of their parents depends upon the resources available to their parent(s). These options for placing children appear to be related to the sex, race, and ethnicity of their mothers, fathers, and other caretakers. National data on state prisoners reveals that 90 percent of the children of male inmates were likely to be placed or remain with their mothers as result of the imprisonment of their fathers (Snell 1994). For children of female inmates, incarceration of the mother was much more disruptive. Upon imprisonment of their mothers, 25 percent of the children were living with their fathers, 51 percent with grandparents, 20 percent with other relatives, 9 percent in foster care, and the balance in other placements (Beck and Gilliard 1995; Snell 1994). Most of these living arrangements reflected a change in where children were living before and during the incarceration of their mothers.

### RESEARCH ON INMATES AS MOTHERS

Research on where children live while their mothers are incarcerated is limited. The studies that have been completed provide some important information about the impact that incarceration has, not only on the inmate but on her family, as well. Many of these studies focus on a particular aspect of the relationship between inmate mothers and their children while incarcerated and after release. Studies reviewed here include information on where children live while their mothers are incarcerated. These are summarized in table 1. One

Table 1. Living Arrangements of Children of Inmate Mothers:
Summary of Research Reports (expressed as percentages)

| Placements of Children | Henriques (1982) (N=75) | Stanton (1980) (N=54) | Bloom & Steinhart (1993) (N=866) | Fessler (1991) (N=111) | Johnston (1995b) (N=500) |
|---|---|---|---|---|---|
| Husband | 8.0 | 22 | 17.4 | 6.3 | 13.2 |
| Grandparents | 48.0 | 35 | 46.6 | 70.3 | 20.4 |
| Maternal | 36.0 | | 38.4 | 53.2 | 9.1 |
| Paternal | 12.0 | | 8.2 | 17.1 | 11.3 |
| Relative | 19.0 | 23 | 18.5 | | 36.0 |
| No state payment | | | | | 23.0 |
| Foster care | | | | | 13.0 |
| Foster care Strangers | 19.0 | 10 | 7.3 | 10.8 | 26.3 |
| Other | 5.7 | 10 | 10.2 | 12.6 | 4.1 |

study by Bresler and Lewis (1986) does not include placement information on children but features an important discussion of racial and ethnic differences in family support for female inmates.

*Henriques.* In her study of how inmate mothers envisioned motherhood, Henriques (1982) interviewed thirty imprisoned mothers and fifteen of their children, along with caretakers in the community and institutional staff. With the exception of one white woman, all respondents were women of color (73 percent black and 23 percent Puerto Rican). The vast majority of these children were in relative care (65 percent), with fewer than 20 percent in state care. Women in this sample were strongly opposed to placing children in state care, yet also expressed concerns about the caretaking by relatives, in terms of their other responsibilities, age and health, and strain upon the relationship. In other words, placements with kin were not trouble free. Mothers expressed concerns about their relationships with their children and about maintaining their place in the home—that is, not being pushed out of their mother position while they were incarcerated. Caretakers and correctional staff characterized mothers as much less committed to and less capable of performing the role of mother than did inmate mothers themselves.

*Stanton.* Stanton's (1980) research examined the impact imprisonment had on the children of inmate mothers. Among areas investigated were changes in the child's living arrangement, school performance, legal socialization, and welfare status. This study compared children whose mothers were in prison with children whose mothers were on probation. Inmate children experienced more changes in residential placement and in school attendance than did children of mothers on probation. Many of the mothers interviewed were misinformed about details in the lives of their children and unaware of some of the difficulties they faced in school and in the community. The living arrangements of 118 children of 54 inmate mothers were as follows: 35 percent with grandmother, 22 percent with father, 23 percent with other relatives, 10 percent in foster care, and the balance in a mix of placements. While Stanton reported an ethnic and racial breakdown of the sample (32 percent white, 48 percent black, and 20 percent Hispanic), she did not report placements by race.

*Bloom and Steinhart.* Focusing on policy implications of the increased imprisonment of women, Bloom and Steinhart (1993) surveyed 430 women about their 866 children, along with correctional staff, caseworkers, and caretakers of children. Bloom and Steinhart found that despite the rapid increase in the population of incarcerated women, few programs had been developed to strengthen the ties between mothers and children during their imprisonment. Sixty-six percent of inmate mothers were members of minority groups, and many were living in poverty. Over half of the sample had not been visited by their children while they were incarcerated, in spite of the fact that 75 percent intended to live with their children after release. The great majority of caretakers surveyed (93 percent) reported that contact with the mother was helpful for the child. The authors examined the role of inmate mothers, caretakers, child welfare, and correctional authorities in addressing the needs of children, and they suggested the development of programs specifically designed to help this population. They reported a placement breakdown similar to that of other studies: 47 percent with grandparents, 17 percent with the father; 18 percent with other relatives; 7 percent in foster care; and 10 percent with friends or other arrangements.

*Fessler.* Fessler's (1991) study of fifty mothers examined reunification plans developed by inmate mothers and followed mothers into the community for a second interview. Although most mothers planned to live with their children upon release from prison, few had prepared detailed plans to accomplish this. During incarceration of their mothers, only 6 percent of the children were living with the father; 17 percent lived with the father's family, 53 percent with the mother's family; 11 percent were in foster care; and 9 percent lived with the mother's friends. Four percent of these children had been adopted. Fessler reported that after release, 73 percent of the mothers were reunited with their children. The population was 52 percent white, 30 percent African American, and 18 percent Hispanic.

*Johnston.* In a more recent report, Johnston (1995b) studied the child-custody problems of 160 male and 500 female inmates. She found that children of male inmates were less likely to experience disruption in living arrangements. However, she reported a much lower percentage of male prisoners' children with their mothers than other studies. This was attributed to the increasing imprisonment of these women. In this study, foster care was used by families when both parents were imprisoned. For children of female inmates, Johnston found that 20 percent were with grandparents, 13 percent were with fathers, 36 percent were with relatives, 26 percent were in foster care, and 4 percent were in other living arrangements.

Most significantly, Johnston discovered that mothers stated that the more troublesome placements were not with foster care but with relatives other than maternal grandparents. This suggests that mothers exerted more power and influence in managing relationships with foster care and with their own mothers than they did in some other relative arrangements. Johnston did not examine the placement data by race and ethnicity, nor was the racial makeup of the population disclosed.

These studies of where children live while their mothers are incarcerated show some interesting differences in the placement resources inmate mothers have at their disposal for child care. Overall, grandparents appear to be the most frequent providers of care for these children, with other relatives also an important resource. Husbands and foster care with nonrelatives or strangers provide less care. The reasons for the varying utilization of these resources are complex. One factor that has not received sufficient attention is the impact of race and ethnicity and class on the placement of children.

THE IMPACT OF RACE AND ETHNICITY ON CHILD PLACEMENTS

There are some studies that do report the relationship between the race and ethnic characteristics of women inmates and where children live. These are summarized in table 2. According to data collected in a comprehensive 1991 survey of women in state prison and jails, race and ethnicity of inmate mothers appeared to be linked with differential use of placements for children (Snell 1994). White children were more likely to live with fathers (35 percent) than were black (19 percent) or Hispanic (24 percent) children. Grandparents were more likely to be the caretakers of black children (57 percent) and Hispanic children (55 percent) than of white children (41 percent),

*Table 2. Living Arrangements of Children by Race and Ethnicity:*
*Summary of Research Reports (expressed as percentages)*

| | Snell (1994) (N=4000) | | | Baunach (1985)* (N=285) | | |
| | White | African American | Hispanic | White | African American | |
| --- | --- | --- | --- | --- | --- | --- |
| Grandparents | 41 | 57 | 55 | 23 | 51 | |
| Other relatives | 15 | 24 | 23 | 23 | 29 | |
| Father | 35 | 19 | 24 | 29 | 10 | |
| Nonrelatives (foster, friends, institutions, and alone) | 22 | 13 | 15 | 25 | 10 | |

| | Zalba (1964)** (N=460) | | | Glick & Neto (1977)*** (N=4263) | | |
| | White | African American | Hispanic | White | African American | Hispanic |
| --- | --- | --- | --- | --- | --- | --- |
| Grandparents | | | | 28 | 56 | 45 |
| Other relatives | 50 | 74 | 58 | 34 | 30 | 31 |
| Father | 25 | 6 | 13 | 17 | 4 | 13 |
| Nonrelatives (foster, friends, institutions, and alone) | 25 | 10 | 29 | 21 | 10 | 11 |

*Using a chi-square test, Baunach found the differences in placements by race to be statistically significant (p<.001).

**Zalba combines grandparents and other relatives in the "other relatives" category. Data on placement with fathers was imputed here from information provided in her research.

***Glick and Neto's study included 214 women who were Native American or other race. These cases are excluded from this table. Ethnic differences in child-care arrangements were significantly different at p=<.001.

and white children were twice (12.6 percent) as likely to be in foster care as other children (6 percent for black and Hispanic children). This statistical report did not suggest any reasons that might explain these racial and ethnic differences in placements.

*Baunach.* One work that did include a racial and ethnic breakdown of placements looked at the impact of mother's imprisonment on both mothers and children. This study examined the living arrangements of 285 children of 190 mothers incarcerated in two states, Kentucky and Washington (Baunach 1985). Half of the mothers in the study were African American and the other half white. Children of white women were more likely than children of African American women to be placed in foster care (25 percent versus 10 percent); black children were more likely to be placed in the care of grandparents (51 percent versus 34 percent) and in the care of other relatives (29 percent versus 23 percent); and white children were more likely to be placed with their father (25 percent versus 10 percent). Although these differences were reported as statistically significant, Baunach did not examine factors that may have contributed to these.

*Glick and Neto.* In a nationwide study of services and programs for incarcerated women, Glick and Neto (1977) assessed the needs of and programs available to incarcerated women. Their research found that although 80 percent of the population had children under the age of eighteen, only about 56 percent of these parents were living with their children prior to the time the women were imprisoned. They also reported that the likelihood of mothers living with their children decreased with each subsequent incarceration. Glick and Neto's survey of over forty-four hundred respondents found a statistically significant difference in living arrangements for children depending on the race and ethnicity of their mothers. Despite the significance of this finding, the researchers did not speculate on the reasons for the divergent patterns of placement.

*Zalba.* Zalba (1964) also reported the differential use of placements for children of 460 white, African American, and Mexican mothers. Only 10 percent of the African American women relied on foster care, compared to 25 percent of the whites and 29 percent of the Mexican

Americans. Similarly, 74 percent of the African American women used relatives other than the father for placements, compared to 50 percent of the whites and 58 percent of the Mexican Americans. Unlike most others writing in this area, Zalba questioned these differences.

> This fact poses questions for consideration. Is it that the internal sub-cultural values of Negroes militate against placing children outside the family? Or is the status quo more closely related to the differential availability of social services, including foster care facilities, depending on the client's ethnic characteristic? (1964, 188)

Zalba's observations are especially important, as they bring to the surface some significant issues about cultural and structural determinants of where children live.

*Bresler and Lewis.* Bresler and Lewis (1986) examined the impact of family ties on black and white female inmates and found sharp differences in the incarcerated population with respect to a variety of family demographics and dynamics. Although the authors were interested in family-related issues, no data were presented on the placement of children. Black women were more likely to have been raised in single-parent female-headed homes (62 percent), while white women's families of origin were more likely to be two-parent families (95 percent). In this sample, only 20 percent of the white women were living with their children prior to incarceration, compared to 54 percent of the black mothers. Only 20 percent of the white women expected help from their family after their release, while a majority (54 percent) of black women reported that help would be forthcoming. Additionally, white women identified available family help by naming only one sibling or a parent, while black women detailed a wider network of help, with potential assistance from aunts, cousins, grandparents, and in-laws, in addition to parents and siblings.

Bresler and Lewis (1986) suggested that, for black women, families provided an extensive source of support and that imprisonment did not bring with it factors of isolation that seemed to accompany the incarceration of white women. White women's estrangement from their families pushed them to rely to a greater extent on boyfriends, casual contacts, and other sources of support. Although the authors did not provide detailed data on the placement of children in their research, they did find important differences in the family resources available to white and black women. They were silent about whether the lack of services from foster care may, in fact, be affecting the patterns of placement for African American and Hispanic children, as suggested by Zalba (1964).

Some clear patterns emerge from these four studies: African American and Hispanic women were more likely to rely on grandparents and other relatives for child placement than were white women, and white women more typically relied on husbands and foster care. Although these research studies were conducted over a thirty-year period and with samples that ranged from less than three hundred women to more than four thousand, the existence of common patterns may reflect some significant differences in the population that have not been directly explored by scholars. What accounts for these differences in placement by race and ethnicity, and what impact do these differences have on how women think about and do "motherhood" on the inside? As shown below, the incarceration event itself brings into sharp focus the possibilities, limitations, and expectations associated with making child-care arrangements for children. The response of families to incarceration of an inmate mother and her ability to enlist, accept, or reject care from kin reveals important and significant differences among women and their families. Some of these differences reflect racial and ethnic differences in family forms. These differences may also be evidenced in the means and paths by which women enter into crime.

## WOMEN, FAMILIES, AND CRIME

As a result of incarceration, inmates confront several challenges and suffer what Sykes (1958) refers to as the "pains of imprisonment." For men, this pain revolves around loss of freedom, autonomy, personal security, heterosexual relationships, and the deprivation of goods and services that can be found in the larger society. For women, the pains of imprisonment revolve around family relations, specifically separation from children (Henriques 1982; Kiser 1991; Neto and Bainer 1983; Stanton 1980), the loss of the maternal role, and, possibly, the legal termination of her rights to her children (Haley 1982). The loss of maternal duties and roles is especially difficult for women who are concerned about the whereabouts and well-being of their children.

Separation of mothers and children is likely to cause significant problems for children, especially those from families who have little familiarity with the criminal justice system and those who are children of first-time offenders (Lowenstein 1986). Mothers who had lived with their children prior to incarceration and assumed major responsibility for their care were often the most distressed and least satisfied with the care provided for their children, whether this was given by foster parents, relatives, or spouses. Dissatisfaction was especially prevalent if that meant disruption in the child's living arrangement. In some instances, mothers had voluntarily given responsibility for children to other relatives. However, in other cases, relatives had moved into the central child-care role in the absence of the mother's performing her mothering responsibilities to their satisfaction (Hunter 1984).

Some research notes that despite criminal involvement and incarceration, inmate mothers are as committed to values associated with parenting as a comparison group of noncriminal mothers on welfare (LeFlore and Holston 1989). Other literature notes that some inmates are conflicted about motherhood and their ability be good parents for their children. These women had become mothers at an early age and had delegated responsibility for the care of their children to older females in their families or had relied on foster care for long-term child care. They had also persisted in criminal lifestyles throughout early adulthood (Thornburg and Trunk 1992). The simple fact of giving birth and having family ties did not, as some might theorize, signal the end or diminution of a criminal career for many in this population (Daly 1987).

The availability of suitable living arrangements for children is of concern not only to the incarcerated woman but also to her family, child-welfare authorities, and others involved in her treatment and custody. In many instances, child welfare will place a child with the inmate's family if that family appears suitable and stable. However, these arrangements may be haphazard if they are made at the time of arrest. In some cases, potential caretakers are already overburdened with other child care and other family responsibilities and may have limited resources to extend to additional children in crisis (Dressel and Barnhill 1994). Grandparents taking care of children of drug-addicted mothers find themselves economically, psychologically, and emotionally exhausted, with few sources of support from other kin or from public and private agencies. This is especially the case for grandparents living in communities that have been negatively affected by drug trafficking and high levels of crime (Burton 1992). In the absence of support services for family care providers, children run the risk of being cared for by kin who are under extreme stress and who may be unable to provide quality child care (Hungerford 1996). Foster care, often the least desirable placement from the point of view of mothers in crisis like addicted or inmate mothers, may provide better care for some children, in terms of financial resources and time and attention from caretakers, than do placements with relatives and family members (Gaudin and Sutphen 1993).

Limited as it is, the research on mothers in prison usually recommends increased visitation between mothers and children to facilitate reunification and to maintain mother-child bonds. In some cases, it is argued that enhancing the connections between mothers and their children will lead to improved chances of the mother's not returning to prison (Showers 1993). One of the shortcomings of this research is that it assumes that all inmate mothers are equally connected to their roles as mothers. For some mothers, plans for reunification are unrealistic and vague rather than doable and specific; and some mothers may view incarceration as a respite from family responsibilities and may not be interested in visitation during incarceration (Hairston 1991). In one of the few research studies that examined inmate mothers' commitment to and performance of mothering, Martin (1997) followed a group of mothers five years after release to track relationships between mothers and their children. In this study, approximately 66 percent of the mothers maintained relationships with their children that the author characterized as "connected." After incarceration, these "connected" inmate mothers resumed or adopted major responsibilities for child care and maintained custody of their children over a five-year period. However, during this period, approximately one-third of the population had lost custody of their children. The mothers' legal rights to the children had been terminated by the court, and many of these children had been adopted.

Several characteristics distinguished connected and noncustodial mothers. Connected mothers were more likely to have supportive relationships with the caretakers of their children, were less likely to have involvement with substance abuse, and were less likely to engage in criminal activity after release. Noncustodial mothers were more likely to suffer from chronic drug dependence and to persist in criminal behavior; they were less likely to have had significant relationships with their children prior to incarceration. As Martin (1997) noted, although the great majority of women expressed the wish to be mothers and to be reunited with their children, for many this desire was seriously compromised by their inability to provide stable and consistent care for their children due to serious involvement with substance abuse and crime.

### PATHS TO PRISON AND THE PLACEMENT OF CHILDREN

How women offenders are recruited to criminal lifestyles may be related to the sorts of placements arranged for children during the incarceration of their mothers. Several sociological theories have attempted to explain the underrepresentation of women in crime by focusing on women's relationship to the family as a social institution. Social control and containment theorists, like Hirschi (1969) and others (Rosenbaum and Lasley 1990; Toby 1957), argue that the closer and more attached individuals are to family, friends, and schools, the less likely they are to become delinquent. These bonds insulate them from the potentially criminogenic factors in their environments and push them to conform more closely to informal means of social control, like gender-specific norms governing conventionality and avoidance of damage to reputation (Heidensohn 1995). Other theorists hold that women's dependence on the family unit maintains social control over their behavior (Kruttschnitt 1981). Women with family responsibilities are less available to commit crimes because of the overarching and powerful responsibilities of child rearing and family maintenance. They are dependent, as well, on the family unit for support, making deviant behavior less likely than it is for men.

Historically, women in conflict with the law were thought to be estranged from their families and to have minimal contact with and support from family and kin. While this theory may have explanatory power concerning some women, it is also important to recognize that family may also provide an important entry and path to crime for women as well. In *Street Woman*, a study of female hustlers, Miller (1986) examined the impact of race and ethnicity on "paths to prison." She suggested that the sources of criminality among black, white, and Hispanic women were quite different and that these differences were closely related to family organization. As Miller reported in her study, responsibilities for child rearing and family support may, in fact, lead women to pursue illegal means to enhance family survival.

While some families may exert the sort of social control theorists suggest, Miller (1986) demonstrated how embedded female offenders were in networks of relationships involving family members. The family, rather than being a protection against a criminal lifestyle, as suggested by Kruttschnitt (1981), in fact may enable and nurture a life of crime. Through family networks access to criminal opportunities, like drug trafficking and hustling, may be as available for some females as it is for males. The embeddedness of criminal opportunities and family networks may make crime-free lifestyles even harder to maintain for women than they are for men (Arnold 1994). According to Miller, access to criminal lifestyles for black women was eased by family members. While the caretakers of young women sought to protect their charges from life on the street, criminal opportunities were afforded by relatives, boyfriends, or other individuals. Miller referred to this as domestic network recruitment.

Access to criminal lifestyles for white women took a different path. These young women, reared in nuclear families, acted out at a young age, ran from parental supervision or maltreatment, and found themselves on the street, where male protectors introduced them to the rigors and attractions of the fast life. Unlike the black women, who maintained contact with both conventional and lawbreaking members of their families and acquaintances, these white women were estranged from their families and not in contact with them. Miller (1986) typed this as the runaway path.

Entering criminal lifestyles to support drug habits characterized paths to lawbreaking for Hispanic women. In this path, women turned to crime after becoming seriously involved with drugs. Miller (1986) noted that white women in her study were more protected from paths to crime than either Hispanic or black women. Black women had all paths open to them—domestic networks, running away, and drug use—while Hispanic women did not have the domestic network path but instead became involved in crime through drug use and running away from home.

Miller (1986) also noted that many of these women were mothers; some of them were involved as principal caretakers of their children, others were helpers to principal caretakers, and still others were estranged from their children and their children's caretakers. White women were more likely to have given children up for adoption or have them placed in foster care. For black women, a child was more often cared for by the child's grandmother or other female members of the family network, an arrangement usually taken for granted.

> There is a clear racial/ethnic difference here. Whites seem not to have developed the pattern of child-keeping characteristic of poor minority members. Even where the mother of a white woman takes care of her daughter's children, the gesture is more likely to be seen as act of generosity than as an unquestioned matter of duty. (1986, 121)

Miller's observation here is an important one, as we will see below.

Since Miller's analysis was published in 1986, there have been additional studies of women's paths to prison or serious involvement in the criminal justice system. In Daly's (1994) study of women in New Haven's felony court, she identified five paths taken by women to serious involvement in the criminal justice system. In her examination, street women accounted for approximately 25 percent of the cases. Other categories included harmed and harming women (38 percent), battered women (13 percent), drug-connected women (15 percent) and other (10 percent), the latter including women without prior arrests or involvement with the criminal justice system. In her deep sample, Daly discovered that most women had alcohol and drug dependencies, half had psychological problems, several had relationships with violent men, and many had family members or boyfriends who were involved in drug sales and use. Although Daly found some differences in the paths taken by white, Latino, and black women, these were not significant.

In her study of jailed women, Richie (1996) examined the impact of race on women's experience with violence in relationships. Comparing differences between black battered women, white battered women, and black women who were not abused, Richie found that black women who were most likely to be abused were those who held unrealistic expectations of relationships and those who were more likely to excuse violence from partners. Richie refers to this as the "gender entrapment model." Battered black women who were more likely to have been the favored child eventually limited their originally high aspirations to attempt to manage abusive relationships and criminal careers. White battered women, on the other hand, saw themselves as the least favored sibling when they were growing up and, as a result, were eager to leave their family of origin. Many experienced abuse in relationships they entered after leaving their own families. Unlike battered black women, white women expressed little family loyalty and connections, characterizing their relationships to family as originating more out of obligation than out of affection.

Black women who had not experienced violence recalled themselves as average children and identified strongly with female caretakers. Their loyalty was more directed to the larger community of black people rather than to members of their families. Unlike battered black women, they did not envision that a relationship with a partner would provide them with a stable, secure life for themselves and their children, and they were, like their mothers, somewhat dismissive of the role of men in their lives. As Richie shows, family membership has significant impacts on whether and how women encounter violence in their relationships and how that may lead to involvement in crime and drug lifestyles. Relying on conjugal relationships appears to be a dangerous strategy of survival for some women, as Richie suggests, especially for certain black women.

In their work on women in conflict with the criminal justice system, Richie, Daly, and Miller all focused on the importance of family in developing criminal careers and in balancing and negotiating family, criminality, and addiction. For women with children, these connections become even more complex. With a criminal justice policy designed for dangerous repeat offenders applied across the board to nonviolent criminals, we can expect that increasing numbers of women and their children will suffer the consequences of a war against drugs and the poor. Documenting the impact of these policies was an important impetus in undertaking the present study.

MANAGING MOTHERHOOD IN PRISON

This research had its origins in fieldwork done at a women's correctional facility in the northeastern United States. As of midyear 1999, this facility housed an average daily population of approximately 250 inmates, 190 sentenced and 60 awaiting trial. The state has no beds that are classified maximum security. Female inmates are housed in two buildings that formerly served as hospitals for the mentally ill. All inmates who are sentenced to serve a sentence are sent to this facility, as there are no local jails.

Access to the prison was made possible by the warden of the facility. As a volunteer and researcher in a prison-based parenting program, I spent time with mothers and their children in an extended visiting program. My initial interest was in learning about the operation of the parenting program, but after a few months at the site my focus moved to how women inmates managed motherhood while incarcerated. My interest in questions that surfaced during the fieldwork led me to the second stage of research, which involved twenty-five in-depth interviews with inmate mothers. The research methodology following the general outline of grounded theory (Charmaz 1983: Strauss and Corbin 1990) is fully explained in the afterword.

These interviews, together with extensive field notes, provided the basis for the research findings. In my analysis, five major strategies emerged as central foci for the management of motherhood in prison. These included arranging and managing caretakers, demonstrating fitness as mothers to official agencies and other audiences, managing motherhood tasks and identities, negotiating ownership of and rights to children, and balancing motherhood, crime, and drug abuse. These five challenges revealed the very real differences between inmate mothers in the management of motherhood. As shown in the following chapters, these are not the result of imprisonment alone but reflect important cultural, class, and racial/ethnic distinctions in the meaning and enactment of motherhood across the social landscape.

SUMMARY

The major aim of this book is to understand how mothers manage motherhood while incarcerated and to arrive at a deeply textured examination of how women inmates understand and enact mother-hood and mothering in this setting. Here, the voices of inmate mothers talking about mothering in prison are given center stage. As noted by many scholars, mothering under any circumstances is challenging. Doing mothering while in prison becomes a nearly impossible task, given the constraints of the setting and given what we as a culture suggest mothers should be and do with respect to their children.

Like other arrangements that must be made by families in crises, determining where children will live is an important one. Here the incarceration event was examined as if it were an independent variable. Where children live while their mothers are incarcerated reveals important dynamics in family organization, not just in individual families but in the location of those families in larger cultural and social milieus. By investigating this population, I contend, it is possible to reveal some of the social forces affecting families in contemporary America, especially as these relate to race and ethnicity. If some families are more ready to accommodate children during the imprisonment of their mothers, what does this reveal about the elasticity and inelasticity of families? What are mothers and others are expected to do vis-à-vis these children while the mothers are incarcerated? How are family obligations and expectations, the placement of children, and the management of motherhood related to how women think and enact motherhood while incarcerated?

In chapter 2, I will review the literature on motherhood and family and suggest how race and ethnicity are related to conceptualizing motherhood within and apart from families. I will also discuss the particular challenges inmate mothers face in doing motherhood and in claiming identities as mothers in a correctional setting. Chapters 3, 4, and 5 examine how women manage motherhood from the inside and how managing motherhood fashions mother trajectories or careers. These chapters make extensive use of the interviews done with inmate mothers. In the final chapter, I will summarize the findings and conclusions based on this examination and discuss implications of this work for policy and program development. In the afterword, I review the research methodology and discuss challenges of conducting research in a women's prison.

# Chapter 2

# The Challenge of Mothering on the Inside

Until recently, little attention was paid to women as offenders in the criminal justice system. As a result, much of the theorizing done in criminal justice, and much of the programming as well, has incorporated a male model (Belknap 1996). This model suggests that gender makes little difference in theorizing and that analysis need not accommodate women as a special category. Although purporting to be gender-free, most of the theorizing about criminality has been inadequate to explain crime, or the relative lack thereof, committed by women (Smart 1976). Recently, feminist scholars and others have begun to investigate and critique the relationships among gender, race, family, and the criminal justice system (Daly and Chesney-Lind 1988; Heidensohn 1987; Leonard 1982). Among the issues feminist theorists have taken up are those related specifically to women offenders and the importance of family; they argue that incarceration of women presents different challenges for women inmates and their families than it does for the men who comprise the vast majority of prisoners. In this chapter, I will review the literature that examines how women manage motherhood in the light of family obligations and how mother identity is affected by the doing of mothering. Of special importance here is how mothers under stress, like those in prison, manage motherhood.

Managing a criminal lifestyle that may lead to incarceration becomes problematic for some women, especially those with children. Confinement to prison presents inmate mothers with several important challenges, the major one being the placement of children. A variety of living arrangements are potentially available for these children. For example, children may live with fathers, with grandparents, or with other kin (including sisters, aunts, friends, and others), or be in foster care. However, the options actually available to individual women for the placement of their children are constrained by a number of factors. Women may find their families are undesirable or unavailable as caretakers; husbands and boyfriends may not be available or be considered not competent to care for children. For some women, the prospect of placing a child in foster care is an option of last resort, one that will not be freely selected by women but one that may be imposed after all other alternatives have been exhausted. The placement of children illuminates how resources—family and other—are deployed during incarceration and how these choices and options are affected by race, ethnicity, and class.

As noted in the previous chapter, there are clear racial and ethnic differences between women in the resources they use to take care of children while they are incarcerated. This chapter will examine what the literature says about how women do motherhood, how family and the state are enlisted to assist them in periods of family crisis, how family obligations are enacted in these settings, and how women manage mother identity as inmates. Race and ethnicity assume a central position here.

## MOTHERHOOD: BEING AND DOING

Because mothering is done in the context of family, ideas about family (including its internal relationships and its relations to other institutions) are essential to understanding how ideas about motherhood evolve and take root. There are several elements of the dominant family ideology. These include: (1) all family members co-reside in a single unit, (2) the family is headed by a male who provides essential economic support to the conjugal unit, (3) socialization of family members into appropriate gender roles is essential (Thorne 1992; Thurer 1994), (4) the interests of all family members are unitary and relations within the family are harmonious, and (5) families are economically self-sufficient, take care of their members, and are not dependent on the state or on extended family members (Bould 1993; Cheal 1991). This dominant model of "the family" puts nonconforming families at a disadvantage, subjecting them to regulation and extensive social control (Donzelot 1979; Smith 1993).

Family ideology sets the stage for prescriptive discourses on motherhood and mothering (Ehrenreich and English 1978). Prescriptive works reflect implicit assumptions about the function of the mother in the larger social context and mothering as practice; this ideology is also called the "mothering discourse" (Griffith and Smith 1987), "intensive mothering" (Hays 1996) and the "myth of motherhood" (Oakley 1976). Prescriptive texts, such as *Dr. Spock's Baby and Child Care* (Spock 1988) and Penelope Leach's *Baby and Child: From Birth to Age Five* (1988), few of which are rooted in sound research, place impossible demands on mothers. Mothering discourse includes the following: (1) mothers are completely engaged with their priceless children and totally absorbed by this work; (2) mothering takes priority over all other work and is the ultimate fulfillment for women; (3) mothers are all-powerful and direct the development and future of their children, and a failure here will place the future of children at risk (Caplan and Hall-McCorquodale 1985); (4) only certain caretakers—namely, biological or adoptive mothers—can "mother"; (5) mothers face motherhood with adequate time and resources; (6) mothers qua mothers perform the emotion work necessary to maintain "happy" families; and (7) with respect to mothering, race and class account for little (Marshall 1991; Phoenix and Woollett 1991). These premises are so prevalent and so implicit that they appear "natural," as the way mothers "should be." This "naturalness" conceals the fact that motherhood is socially produced and constructed; that mothering is the result of effort and practice, of deliberate actions and agency; and that these are located in specific social, economic, and historic contexts (Ambert 1994; Glenn 1987; Zinn 1994).

MOTHERHOOD AND MOTHERING AS POSITION,
RELATIONSHIP, AND ACTIVITY

Being a mother and doing motherhood present an array of complex situations for all mothers. As feminist researchers and theoreticians have pushed scholars to examine or deconstruct motherhood apart from ideological naturalized understandings, a few empirically

based works have begun to inform theories about motherhood and
the tasks associated with caretaking and mothering.

Although there has been considerable research in the past decade
on the doing and meaning of housework, there has been less research
about other forms of household work, like food preparation and
caretaking of children. DeVault's (1991) study of "feeding the family"
carefully illustrates how family work is deeply weighted with symbolic significance and how meanings associated with this type of
caretaking vary across social class and racial groups. In contrast to simple
preparation of food for family members, "feeding the family" carries
meanings associated not only with caregiving but with gender and the
acting out of caretaking relationships. The disparity of resources that
confronts women in putting food on the table contributes to varying
interpretations of what should be done in feeding one's family (the
ideology) and what can be done (the actual doing and struggling to
accomplish this work). DeVault's research sensitizes investigators of
the family and mothering to be particularly aware of the variety of
meanings attached to this work, because these have important implications for reinforcing and reproducing female identity and status. In
the case of inmate mothers, we need to pay attention to the differing
levels of resources available to them, as well as to the tasks performed
by mothers who are away from their children and attempting to complete instrumental and affective mother work.

More complex than either housework or feeding the family is care
for children. Increasingly, children are being placed in the care of substitute care providers. Some important research has examined how
day-care providers and mothers negotiate child care and ideas about
mothering and children. Nelson (1994) interviewed day-care providers to examine the complex relations between mothers and the women
who care for their children. The positioning of mothers in conventional understanding as "owners" of children puts other providers and
caretakers in less-privileged positions. Day-care providers claim their
mothering of children even when the mothers of children do not recognize or appreciate these connections. The meanings attached to
mothering other women's children surface as women make distinctions between emotion work directed to one's own children and to
those for whom one's attachment is made by the day-care contract.

Uttal (1994) studied mothers who placed their young children in the care of day-care providers, as well. The central question posed in this investigation was how mothers maintain identities as mothers when others are providing the bulk of daily care for their children. Uttal found that relationships between mothers and day-care providers could be characterized in one of three ways. First, some mothers regard day care as "supervision" or enrichment, and as not interfering at all with their mothering relationship with their children. In this interpretation, which Uttal typed as "custodial," mothers make clear distinctions between the care they provide to children as mothers and the caretaking others give, suggesting that it is in their care that children receive real mothering. A second group of respondents suggest that they and day-care providers share the mothering of children and provide "coordinated care"; both care providers are seen as mothering the child. Finally, some mothers regard day care as "relinquished" mothering, suggesting that the day-care providers give children "real" mothering and that their own roles are more peripheral. These distinctions both support traditional concepts of motherhood (that is, only one individual can mother—suggested by custodial and relinquishment models) and challenge them (that is, that several caretakers can mother children and that all have claim to significant relationships with children, reflected in coordinated care). These findings also suggest that doing good mothering and believing that one was a good mother can take place in a variety of child-care arrangements and need not always involve the child's mother in constant, unique, and singular care of the child. Research on day care and substitute care providers sheds light on how mother work is manifested in relationships with care providers and in managing ownership of children. These issues—managing relationships with care providers and constructing claims to children—are also salient for inmate mothers.

McDonald's (1998) work on manufacturing motherhood examines children in the care of nannies and au pairs. In this relationship, working professional-class mothers negotiate with child-care providers from a position of power. The differences between women in access to power and resources and the conditions under which child care is managed are important. Women who employ others to take care of their children can set conditions of care and can reserve for themselves tasks that are considered high status. Women with less status and power are often deprived of the ability to set forth conditions of care. As a group, inmate mothers are frequently in a position of little power and influence, even over the lives of their own children. In addition to their lack of material resources, their capability to insist on high-quality care for their children in undermined by their removal from the community and by their status.

In research focusing on how becoming a mother transforms women, McMahon (1995) found that motherhood is enacted and actively constructed by women and is not a simple matter of gender socialization. Motherhood is distinguished from other social commitments, not only by how much is committed but by what is committed to parenthood. Chief among these commitments is the ultimate responsibility for children. McMahon suggests that this commitment of ultimate responsibility is rendered equivalent to a mother's moral worth. Most interestingly, McMahon argues that being a mother (the status) and doing mothering (the taking on and adequate performance of tasks) are quite separate notions. Because of its romanticized quality, the identity of "mother" provides women with special status even when their performance of tasks associated with the role is less than skillful. Inmate mothers' connections with children as their mothers but not their caretakers clearly expresses the difficulty of claiming identity as a "good mother" when others have responsibility for children.

In her research on how women conceptualize motherhood, Hays (1996) found that women respond to various ideologies about raising children and select from a number of sources to account for their own mothering styles.

> Mothers make selections among these sources and develop interpretations based on their social circumstances—including both their past and present social positions and their past and present cultural milieu. . . . Individual mothers, therefore, actively engage in reshaping social ideology of appropriate child rearing. This process means that every mother's understanding of mothering is in some sense unique. It also means that there are systematic group differences among mothers that are grounded in their different social positions and different cultural worlds. (1996, 74)

For inmate mothers, we can expect that ideas and performance of some mothers will be different from that of other mothers because of different social and cultural worlds. As Smart notes, ideals about what a good mother is supposed to do and be are "class specific, historically located" (1996, 45). While mothers may resist these ideologies about the perfect mother and good mothering, the dominant discourse makes it difficult for mothers to sustain mothering practices that are alternative to the mainstream. Some of these struggles to do mothering are the result of differences in resources that lead to differences in strategies used to do this mother work (Garey 1995). This means that inmate mothers will construct mothering in prison with a variety of ideas about what constitutes good mothering, along with an array of strategies to accomplish this.

Mothering, of course, is not done separately from families and ideas about family. Not only are ideas about mothering powerful, but cultural ideals about family form are also prevalent and influential. Mainstream social scientists have characterized the extended family as an artifact of earlier societies that would disintegrate because it was not suited to modern economies (Goode 1964; Parsons 1964). However, research has demonstrated that extended family relationships have persisted, even while the idealized nuclear family has weakened. Relationships among kin and fictive kin provide mutual support to households and improve chances of survival (Peterson 1993). Extended networks of providers stretch limited resources and incorporate a number of adults in the caretaking of children (Stack 1974). The development of "othermothers" (Collins 1990), fictive kin, and permeable family boundaries challenges dominant definitions of bounded nuclear units and also calls into question some of the assumptions about the roles and positions of mothers in caretaking. Although some research indicates that these exchanges are rooted in economic need, other research shows that kin contact and exchange persist even when economic crises are no longer prevalent. This seems especially to be the case in exchanges among racial and ethnic minorities where networks of support continue independent of income (Raley 1995). Relationships with family have significant impacts for how women construct motherhood in specific settings and situations. These constructions of motherhood are deeply embedded in definitions of family and family obligations.

How women construct motherhood and mothering is an active process and very much dependent on how "family" is defined in particular contexts. Whom one defines as family members differs significantly across race, ethnicity, and class. Determining who "family" is exists as an important and critical task for family members, one that has long-range importance and significance for managing and interpreting performance and identity as members. As Finch (1989) and others have argued, the role of the family as a resource and as an institution has diminished in contemporary Western societies. Functions previously performed by family are now executed by the state or by the private market (Hays 1996).

Whether one relies on family depends on structural factors (social and cultural norms about what is obligated) and on negotiated commitments within families. Systems of exchange within families are very much a matter of social construction that occur within larger systems in the social structure. For example, while some families may welcome the birth of a child to a unwed seventeen-year-old daughter, other families are less likely to offer assistance and more likely to suggest termination of the pregnancy if at all possible. Similarly, what for some families is a tragedy, such as the incarceration of a son for possession of drugs, is more an unfortunate circumstance for other families. What is expected of a unmarried, working-class son of an Alzheimer's patient may be different from what is expected of her married, middle-class daughter. The obligations that family members have in response to these events are a result of larger systems of public morality and within-group norms of what constitutes appropriate behavior and obligations among members.

Given this broad explanatory framework, we could expect families to respond to member needs in a variety of ways, governed by large structural factors and race, class, gender, and other subgroup identifiers. However, because much of family work is hidden from view, it is not easy to discover the rules that govern exchanges within families. These may not come into play until a crisis surfaces, revealing patterns of obligations that are enacted as a response to the event (Gubrium and Holstein 1990). These patterns of obligation are surfaced as inmate mothers face incarceration.

A variety of principles and considerations govern the exchange of help. These include: (1) the quality of the relationship between the parties, (2) the history of exchanges among the members, (3) the impact of help on the development of a dependency relationship, (4) the life course of the family, and (5) the determination that help is appropriately exchanged at the time. Finch (1989) argues that exchange and family obligations operate in a larger context but are also the result of enacted understandings among family members. Accounts of obligations must be given to external and internal audiences, as well. In other words, not only is help exchanged (or not) but reasons for these actions must be presented to others who can determine compliance with normative obligations. Whether or not family members respond to inmate mothers' needs for child care depends upon relationships within families prior to incarceration, whether family members have provided help before in a way that led to successful resolution of the crisis, whether members are able to assist, and whether or not taking care of children while their mother is in this sort of crisis—that is, incarceration—is normatively expected in particular contexts.

Ideas about family are created and recreated over the life course and across situations; and ideas are constantly in flux about who constitutes family and what family members do for each other (Gubrium and Holstein 1990). Discourses about "what family is" are found in multiple contexts, and these reveal much about the patterning of relationships. Because inmate mothers come from a variety of social backgrounds, important differences in how their families work surface among them. The discourses that reveal what families are expected to do are not uniform but instead differ across class, race, ethnicity, and other social groupings.

Three key questions surface in learning how family works. These include: "Who cares?," "Who takes care?," and "For how long?" Burton and Stack (1992) refer to these phenomena as "kinscripts" that have three aspects: kin-work, kin-time, and kinscription. Kin-work refers to the work that families must perform to survive over time. Kin-time corresponds to family ideas about the sequencing and timing of movement into role transitions and positions. These family norms may conform to dominant norms or may reflect ethnic, racial, or cultural norms and values. Kinscription relates to the ways in which family members are enlisted and engaged to do family work. Some members of the family are more readily recruited for family work. As research has demonstrated, women are more frequent caretakers and arrangers of care. Although kin-scripts set forth patterns of expectations among family members, individuals may resist, attempting to change, ignore, or violate scripts. What is important and valuable about kin-scripts is that they provide a sensitizing framework for researchers who are interested in learning how family obligations are enacted across race and class. It is in dealing with these challenges that family emerges. In the case of inmate mothers, the enlistment of resources to care for children illustrates how families' response to crises (or lack of response) is patterned along gendered, racial, and cultural lines.

Relying on family support has been thought to be characteristic of poor communities of color (Martin and Martin 1978; R. J. Taylor 1986). Much of the early work done on kin support was qualitative. exemplified by Carol Stack's oft-cited *All Our Kin* (1974), in which kin and fictive kin operated in networks of mutual support to enhance survival in a black community in the late sixties. Patterns of child keeping emerged to take care of children across households. Children, regarded as resources, were taken care of as a community effort and considered neither a burden nor the sole responsibility of a single parent. A number of scholars have questioned whether these networks retain their viability today. Collins (1994) suggests that networks of blood mothers and othermothers have been weakened in communities under siege by illegal drugs and the accompanying rise in crime. She notes, however, that even in the most distressed communities, female-centered patterns of child care persist. Although there is extensive research on family exchange, findings on the likelihood, type, and extension of family support across race, ethnicity and class remain inconclusive.

## FAMILIES IN CRISIS

Family understandings of bonds and connections become even more acute when taken-for-granted situations are challenged. An event like the incarceration of a female family member poses important questions for a family. If there are children, who among the family members is obligated to take care of these children? Who cares about them? For how long will this caretaking continue? The response of family members to this situation reveals important differences among families across the social structure. Expectations and norms about what family means for white, African American, and Hispanic family members—and for middle-class, working-class, and poor members—may be quite different.

When families confront a crisis, taken-for-granted understandings of obligations are challenged, and new understandings are put into context and enacted. Farber (1964) has provided a general framework to understand how families respond to crises. For Farber, families consist of mutually contingent careers, so that disruption in the expected life pattern of one member has significant impact not only on the family member but on others in the family and on the unit as a whole. In some instances, family members will respond to a crisis, adjust, and resume relations much as they were before the crisis (Hill 1949). In other situations, however, crises may mean the dissolution of the family unit, or expulsion or freezing out of the member precipitating the crisis. If the family member is frozen out, that individual's career is no longer in line with the career of the family, and the individual no longer has to be considered by the rest of the family members.

As Farber recognized, not all potentially disruptive events are viewed as family crises. Imprisonment of a family member may be viewed by some families as a threat, not only to their financial and emotional well-being but to their status and position in the community as well. In other instances, incarceration may be viewed less as a crisis and more as an interruption in routine. As families face crises, they go through multiple stages, requiring that they employ a variety of coping strategies. Depending on the type of crisis, some or all of these strategies may be employed. The most relevant strategy for this discussion relates to the rearrangement of age, sex, and generation roles when family members are incarcerated. For male inmates, this means that wives and members of extended families perform work, like household chores, and offer financial and emotional support previously provided by men (Swan 1981). For women inmates, household management and taking care of children must be arranged as well. As caretakers are enlisted by inmate mothers to care for children, other relatives may assume major responsibility for child care. Husbands and boyfriends may take up many of the tasks previously performed by the mothers. Older children may assume responsibility for supervision of younger children along with household management tasks that were performed by incarcerated mothers. As the member in crisis, the mother's place vis-à-vis the family also changes. Mothers in prison may be assigned a less central role in the family and may themselves become the object of care and supervision. This minding and control of inmate mothers is not only accomplished by correctional institution staff but also by watchful children and caretakers to guarantee that they comply with institutional rules and regulations. As women persist in careers as offenders and addicts and suffer multiple incarcerations, we might expect that their places in families to become more peripheral and, as Farber predicts, the women may become frozen out of family life.

## ORGANIZED RESPONSES TO
## FAMILY PROBLEMS

While Farber's perspective provides an important picture of the family as a self-regulating system, it is important to account for how larger social contexts and gender, race, class, and ethnicity may affect responses to crises. The factors that lead family members to rely upon each other or to enlist outside resources in time of need can be examined in the contexts of specific crises. Solinger's (1992) work on unwed pregnancy in the era preceding widespread access to legalized abortion presents an interesting examination of the divergent paths of organized responses for white and African American girls who found themselves pregnant. Solinger argues that while social services were available for white families through adoption of unwanted children, thereby removing the stigma of illegitimate children, no such programs were available for the children of African American women. The denial of services rested on an ideological understanding that the African American community would "take care of its own," that black babies were not adoptable, and that illegitimacy was not stigmatized in the community. This analysis suggests the deeply raced understanding of illegitimacy in that era that continues to the present. So while families attempt to respond to crises, larger systems that could assist families in crisis may or may not be available to them. Not accounted for in Solinger's work was the possibility that African American families mistrusted mainstream white social service agencies, feared that children would be placed inappropriately and resisted the intrusion of these agencies into their lives. As we examine placement options for children of inmate mothers, we will see how families interact with state authorities to access services or to avoid them. For inmate mothers, the availability of resources for child care is significantly determined by how they view help from family, state agencies, and others.

To explain placement differences for children of inmates from white, African American, and Hispanic families, we need to examine cultural differences about obligations to children across family units and negotiations among family members about obligations. In this interpretation, we might suggest that cultural and social norms that govern family behavior across race and class propel some women to seek help from families. On the other hand, relationships with families push other women to seek assistance from the state child-welfare system or from boyfriends or husbands in the conjugal unit.

The processes by which imprisoned women in families resist and enlist caretaking for their children from family, from the state, and from others provide important insights into how race, class, and gender interact in families.

## MANAGING MOTHERHOOD IN PRISON: IDENTITIES AS MOTHERS

If there are cultural and social differences in expectations about what members of families should do for each other, it can be argued that these differences will also have an impact on how mothers see their roles in families and how they understand their obligations as mothers. Here symbolic interactionism provides a good theoretical grounding. Inmate mothers are, by virtue of their imprisonment, living apart from their children and face a variety of challenges in constructing and maintaining identities and roles as mothers. If an understanding of motherhood and an enactment of mothering depend on social position and on relationships with family, how do women understand these identities, how salient they are, and how those identities are threatened as children are cared for and mothered by others?

For purposes of clarity, it is important to distinguish between several terms that are used somewhat loosely in theoretical discussions about positions, roles, role performances, identities, and self-concepts. Following Goffman (1961), I will refer to positions as statuses and places in the social order, to roles as the activities of incumbents as they act out the normative demands of those positions, and to role performances as the work that particular individuals do in the enactment of roles. Social identity refers here to an individual's feeling that she or he is part of a certain social group or category that carries some emotional significance (Tajfel 1978). Because identities are many and varied and, in some instances, competing and contradictory, individuals must manage to balance identities, with the result that some are more salient, carry more commitment, and have more significant impact on the development of self-concept.

In the case of inmate mothers, we can identify motherhood as a position, inmate motherhood as a role, and the various ways inmate mothers manage motherhood while incarcerated as role performances. As inmate mothers manage motherhood in prison, they strive to construct and maintain mother positions and performance under considerable stress. Even when they perform tasks associated with "good mothering," this does not guarantee that they can claim identities as "good mothers." Mere performance of a role does not constitute identity. As we will see in chapters 3, 4, and 5, to develop identity as a "good mother" her performances must be evaluated and made something of by important audiences, including self, caretakers, child-welfare officials, other mothers, and correctional staff.

How a woman views her parenting role is dependent upon a development of self-identity and how this role compares or contrasts with that of others she views as good mothers (LeFlore and Holston 1989). As both mothers and inmates, women face a number of social situations, the most significant of which will be detailed in the following chapters. An inmate mother needs to arrange and manage caretaking of her children, construct and manage a motherhood role in the context of imprisonment, demonstrate fitness as a mother, negotiate ownership of children, and balance identity and work as mother, criminal, and possibly substance abuser.

An inmate mother's presentation and performance as mother is compromised by virtue of her imprisonment. The mere absence from children calls into question her performance of that role. As an incarcerated mother, the charge of "unfit" mother may be readily attached to her by caretakers, prison officials, child-welfare authorities, family members, the courts, and others (Mahan 1982). In many jurisdictions, the mere fact of imprisonment may constitute abandonment as a ground for legal intervention and the loss of child custody (Genty 1995; Haley 1977; Bloom 1995).

The moral career of an inmate mother follows a trajectory, as suggested by Goffman (1961). Identity as an inmate mother assumes a moral character for two reasons. The first reason is linked to the role and position of mothers in a larger context. Evaluation of performance as a mother is an ongoing process. These evaluations are taken up by self, by interested others, and, in instances where social agencies are involved, by those with credentials to police, evaluate, and control behavior. Because motherhood and mothering are tied to normative evaluations, these are not morally neutral positions and performances.

The moral career takes on a second aspect as well. In the case of imprisoned mothers, women also take up inmate mother identities as they are fashioned with other inmate mothers, in comparison to and in opposition to those identities. Balancing inmate identities with mother identities provides women with complex choices. This is not to say, of course, that these are the only two choices imprisoned mothers have. It is simply to note that these two identities stand in opposition to what are conventionally considered positions as mothers and positions as inmates.

Children are valuable resources in that they are primary validators of inmate mothers' identities as mothers and as women (Day and Mackey 1988; McMahon 1995). On the one hand, the fact of children provides normalizing status. It qualifies an inmate as a "normal" member of the world of females. On the other hand, the fact of children also provides a dilemma in accounting. If she as a good mother is committed to her children, how does she explain her involvement in chronic substance abuse and in activities that led her to incarceration, especially for a series of incarcerations and for lengthy sentences? Most inmate mothers will seek to connect with their position as mothers and detach themselves from their positions as inmates, at least in the early stages of their criminal justice careers.

IDENTITY STRATEGIES

This construction of identity is accomplished through the strategy of "identity talk," which provides a useful way to account for self and to manage negative identities. In their study of the homeless, Snow and Anderson (1987) identified three strategies employed by homeless men and women in constructing positive identities. The first strategy involved distancing oneself from the situation and the setting, namely other homeless individuals and the agencies that serve them, and claiming that one is not "like the rest." In the second strategy, subjects embraced the homeless role and tied it to a larger social end, rejecting mainstream goals and means and identifying other homeless individuals as friends and protectors. Finally, subjects pursued fictive storytelling, denying or exaggerating the past and fantasizing about the future. Each of these strategies suggests resistance to an imposition by the larger society of an identity that is largely held in contempt and regarded with disdain. Use of these identity strategies varied with time on the street. Distancing strategies were more likely to be employed by individuals with brief street careers, while strategies to embrace homeless identity were more characteristic of individuals with longer careers as homeless men and women. The fictive strategy of embellishing the past was used most often by individuals with two to four years of street experience, while fantasizing about the future was adopted by those with six months or less on the street.

For women inmates, who like the homeless occupy a position that is negatively evaluated by the larger society, we may expect that distancing strategies would be employed during first weeks or months of imprisonment and during initial incarcerations. In other words, upon the first incarceration or during the first months of serving a sentence, women inmates seek to distance themselves from other women inmates. Women may claim they that are unlike other inmates because of their special relationships with their children. Upon subsequent incarcerations, women inmates may come to embrace the inmate role or at least become comfortable in returning to prison to be with other individuals they consider as friends and protectors. This can be demonstrated in a variety of ways. Women also embrace the role of inmate while arguing that even in pursuit of a criminal career, children have been taken care of, albeit by another caretaker. As Stanton (1980) showed, many inmate mothers also embellish former relationships with children and family. They also fantasize about their return to the community, imagining they will have adequate housing and loving children and will have conquered severe drug dependency problems.

To maintain identity as a mother, a generally positive and socially sanctioned status, women inmates employ a variety of strategies to defend that identity from threat. Women face threats to identities as mother based on their individual qualities (you are not a good mother!) or by virtue of membership in the category inmate, addict, prostitute, or criminal (good mothers are not addicts, prostitutes, etc.) (Breakwell 1986). These threats to identity are leveled by caretakers, clinicians, children, child-welfare officials, and even by inmates themselves. When positive identities are threatened, individuals attempt to cope in a variety of ways. Women inmates try to deflect attacks by redefining the situation or by denying the situation is a troublesome one (I am a drug user, but that does not affect my children). They compartmentalize the problem and attempt to draw boundaries around these concerns (I am an addict, but my children never knew I used drugs; I kept that from them). Women inmates may also attempt to redefine the situation by attributing imprisonment to being sick and seeking help rather than to being punished for violating a law (I am a better mother in here than I was on the street, because I am getting the help I need). These strategies are deployed on a intrapsychic as well as an interpersonal level as inmate mothers do mothering in prison.

Not all mothers are able to successfully deflect threats to positive mother identity. The attachment of a "bad mother" label may be temporary or permanent. In cases where others are taking care of their children, some inmate mothers will accommodate the threat to identity by accepting the fact that others are only *temporarily* caring for their children. When mothers have lost legal custody of children or have had legal rights to children terminated by the court, typically a permanent change in mother's position vis-à-vis the child, they often contend that the termination of their legal rights to children is the result of an unfair and callous child-welfare system. In many instances, as we will see later, mothers with chronic drug problems and multiple incarcerations, and who have provided intermittent care of children, will eventually find themselves without an active and significant role in raising their children (Hairston 1991). Demonstrating fitness—that is, maintaining and reinforcing links to identities as mothers—becomes a central focus of mother work that inmate mothers do in prison.

## MOTHERHOOD IN PRISON: RACE AND ETHNICITY

For purposes of this discussion, we can look at motherhood as a position that is created by virtue of giving birth or adopting a child; this is different from mothering as an activity or role performance, which is equivalent to doing mothering. While this may provide a convenient conceptualization, it is also important to consider the idea of mothering and motherhood careers. This suggests different levels, paths and conceptualizations of motherhood and mothering on the part of mothers, as suggested by Hays (1996) and Uttal (1994). Mothers evaluate their centrality to their children and their own performance as mothers in a variety of ways. This has important implications for understanding how women in prison may view their position vis-à-vis their children who are with substitute care providers.

Black and Hispanic women are more likely than white women to have prior experience with shared child keeping (Stack 1974; Angel and Tienda 1982; Collins 1990). These settings typically involve shared decision making, common disciplinary philosophies, and significant shared knowledge about children. Child-care patterns that take place prior to incarceration set the stage for the persistence of these arrangements following imprisonment. This shared parenting provides women of color with family and kin who are familiar with and known to the child. For women of color, mothering may be less a private matter than it is for white women. White women, on the other hand, have less experience in these arrangements and are less likely to be able to draw upon family and kin resources who are familiar with their children. Because white families are more privatized and less permeable than are families of color, "ownership" of children is also more privatized (Collins 1990). In this context, concerns about ownership of children distinguish white families from families of color and have important implications for how inmate mothers and caretakers manage relationships.

Similarly, obligations to take care of children in times of crises may be more salient for black and Hispanic families than they are for white families. Caretaking of children by family members may be done out of normative obligation in the case of minority families and out of necessity and with resistance in white families (Bresler and Lewis 1986). As Farber (1964) notes, deviant family members may be frozen out of the family, making family resources unavailable for members in trouble. For women who are estranged from families, reliance upon non-family others for child care may bring them to the attention of child-welfare authorities and bring into question their parenting. If a child is placed in foster care, the mother must often deal with caretakers who are unknown to her. Maintaining a relationship with the child is mediated by the child-welfare authorities and, in most instances, the mother has less personal power than she would have in dealing with family members, husbands, and friends. This is not to say that relationships with relative caretakers are without complications and that one's performance as a mother does not have to be accounted for in these situations. However, in family and conjugal-based caretaking, women do usually have more opportunities to be involved with a child. This provides women with greater latitude within which to negotiate parental involvement.

Role distance provides a useful perspective in examining how women manage motherhood while incarcerated. Role distance is displayed in how mothers enact and perform mother roles while incarcerated. Typically, women attempt to maintain central places in the lives of the children, assigning other caretakers an advisory role, similar to custodial or coordinated care, as suggested by Uttal (1994). Because of the length of their sentences or difficult relations with the caretakers of their children, imprisoned mothers may distance themselves or be distanced from the mother role. Individuals are usually deeply committed, only to roles they perform regularly. If it is expected that an inmate mother will be away from her children for long periods of time because of a lengthy sentence, caretakers will be enlisted for long-term involvement with children. This involves the mother's conceding major and day-to-day decision making to caretakers. If the confinement is a long one and caretakers are not supportive, a temporary assignment may evolve into a permanent involuntary taking of children.

Moving away voluntarily or involuntarily from the mother role and position is not a neutral act like a leaving a job or changing a career. Because motherhood is equated with the moral worth of women, women assume or take on a position of moral excellence by being a good mother (McMahon 1995). This worth is taken for granted until it is called into question, as it may be at imprisonment. As the research indicates, not all women who come to prison have been living with children prior to incarceration (Bloom and Steinhart 1993; McGowan and Blumenthal 1978). Some reports indicate that as many as 30 percent of women in prison were not living with their children at the time of their incarceration ( Snell 1994). Black women were more likely to have been living with children prior to incarceration than were white women (Baunach 1985; Snell 1994). For women whose children are being taken care of by another before incarceration, imprisonment does not bring about the sorts of dislocations that it does for women who were the sole or central care providers for children. Women who have been at the center of caretaking for their children not only must arrange substitute care but must also evaluate the context and quality of that care. In these instances, three possibilities confront inmate mothers. They may consider all that they have done as mothers before incarceration and attempt to replace it by delegating tasks and maintaining primary control. Alternatively, they may opt to assign or concede control to the substitute provider. Finally, they may attempt to negotiate some mother work and position that is somewhere in the middle of these two poles.

As noted above, mainstream mothering discourse proposes that mothers assume a unique and irreplaceable position in the lives of their children, that mothers and only mothers can perform certain duties with respect to children and that mothers and mothers alone can claim attachment to children in unique ways. Because this discourse does not reflect the experience of women of color or women with limited economic means (Collins 1994; Glenn 1994), they may be less likely to embrace this ideology or to use it to guide their construction of what motherhood and mothering mean. White women may be more likely to consider that there are some tasks that only the child's mother can do and that their individual styles of parenting differs from that of their own mothers. Similarly, they may be less likely to believe that there may be adequate substitute providers equal to them. Minority mothers, on the other hand, may be less convinced that they and only they can mother their children. Economic circumstances and cultural preferences provide these mothers with contexts within which to favor shared child keeping. With experience mothering other children as well as their own, black and Hispanic inmate mothers may be less convinced that their absence from their children will of necessity result in irreparable damage to them.

Research also indicates that some women do not have plans to reunite with their children after their release from incarceration. Baunach (1985) found that 20 percent of women inmates did not intend to assume major responsibility for child care after release. This figure was higher for white women than for black women. Some inmate mothers have had rights to their children legally terminated by the courts due to neglect, abuse, or death of a child, or for another reason. Other inmate mothers opt to continue in criminal and drug lifestyles and to have children remain with substitute caretakers. Women who are not taking care of their children, like absentee and noncustodial mothers, may receive nearly universal condemnation from children, the courts, caretakers, other parents, and the general public. Not wanting one's children or admitting that other caretakers are superior may suggest that one is unfit to parent and certainly calls into question one's allegiance to gender mandates. Articulating a wish to reunite with children when one is better able to provide care or suggesting that one is a good mother because one has arranged for others to take care of children may support identity as a "good mother."

Even some mothers who have had children taken away by the courts or had legal rights to children terminated maintain claims to motherhood by virtue of biological connections. But some other inmate mothers maintain that even though they have given birth to certain children, they do not claim a mother connection to them because others have appropriated the mother role. These assessments of relationships reflect the fact that mothers manage and construct mothering relationships with children individually, and do not maintain the same relationship with all of the children born to them.

SUMMARY .

Social positions locate women in structural and cultural sites where family obligations are set forth and negotiated. As noted above, race, class, and ethnicity make a difference in how these family obligations are enacted and acted out. The extent to which family resources can be utilized is an important consideration for inmate women with children. As women attempt to fashion good places for children to live, they are challenged to consider what this may entail. Further, because most will not maintain major day-to-day responsibility for children while they are incarcerated, they are also faced with determining what it means to be a "good" mother while others are taking care of their children. Constructing that role and identity is a matter of work and active negotiation, not only by the inmate mother but by many other parties as well.

In managing motherhood in prison, inmate mothers face significant challenges and social situations. The concepts introduced in this chapter will be examined in the following chapters. What inmate mothers bring to prison in terms of relationships with family, ideas about mothering and child care, paths to prison, race and ethnicity, length of sentences, prior incarcerations, and other dimensions will determine not only how they understand and manage motherhood in prison but also will direct their careers as inmate mothers.

# Chapter 3

# Arranging Care and Managing Caretakers

Studying how inmate mothers manage motherhood provides an opportunity to examine how families respond to crises and how this differs across racial and ethnic groups. While some research has shown that the race and ethnicity of inmate mothers appear to be related to where children live while their mothers are in prison, little is known about how these placements are arranged, how they are managed, and what impacts these differences have on how women manage identity as mothers during incarceration. In this and the two chapters that follow, I will examine how women manage motherhood in prison by investigating responses to five social situations. This chapter will address how women arrange child care and manage caretakers while they are incarcerated. In the process of arranging and managing child care, relationships with caretakers and families set the stage for managing motherhood in prison. The next chapter will explore how inmate mothers demonstrate to others their fitness for motherhood and how inmate mothers and others negotiate the ownership of children. The final chapter will take up how inmate mothers construct motherhood and mothering, and how inmate mothers balance crime, addiction, and motherhood. The social situation of balancing motherhood, crime, and drugs creates challenges for women who are attempting to reestablish places as mothers. These situations have direct implications for the development of mother careers or trajectories.

There are a number of variables that are important to consider when examining the management of motherhood in prison in our sample. These include length of sentence, involvement with child welfare, ages of children, previous histories of incarceration, and others.

43

To consider these dimensions, the sample was chosen to reflect maximum variation (Lincoln and Guba 1985) among the members rather than representativeness of a larger population. These dimensions were considered important factors in the work and tasks associated with managing motherhood in prison. The salience of these dimensions in developing and fashioning women's identities as mothers will be discussed below.

The population selected for investigation here reflects profiles of imprisoned women in other jurisdictions. Of the sample of twenty-five, most (60 percent) were women of color. Ages ranged between twenty-two and forty years of age, with a mean of thirty-two years. On average, women gave birth to three children with the range between one child and six children. Of the seventy-seven children born to these women, two had died and eighteen had been adopted by other parents. Children were between the ages of six months and twenty-one years old. Of this population, 48 percent were serving a first sentence, 36 percent were serving second and third sentences, and 16 percent were chronic offenders, serving more than four terms. (See table 3 for summary statistics on the sample and comparison statistics on the population at the correctional facility).*

Examining how inmate mothers respond to five key social situations makes it possible to see how careers as inmates and mothers emerge and develop. The making of these careers follow trajectories that were fashioned by paths to prison, race and ethnicity, relationships with child-welfare agencies, and other dimensions.

## ARRANGING CARE AND MANAGING CARETAKERS

One of the immediate challenges that face women who are coming to jail or prison is the placement of their children. As noted in chapter 1,

---

*Statistics on the institutional population were obtained from official agency reports and communications with staff. When comparable data was not available from agency sources, information from Snell's (1994) national report on women inmates was used. This was the case for number of children ever born and for living arrangements prior to incarceration. Comparable data on chronic recidivism and ages of children were not available.

## Table 3. Comparison Statistics: Sample and Institutional Population

| | Profile of sample (N = 25) | Percent | Institution Percent |
|---|---|---|---|
| **Race and Ethnicity** | | | |
| White | 10 | 40 | 59 |
| African American | 10 | 40 | 34 |
| Hispanic | 4 | 16 | 7 |
| Native American | 1 | 4 | 0.8 |
| **Age** | | | |
| Range | 22–41 | — | 18–58 |
| Mean years | 32 | — | 32 |
| **Length of sentence** | | | |
| 1 year or less | 10 | 40 | 60 |
| 1 year 1 day to 3 years | 4 | 16 | 23 |
| 3 years 1 day to 10 years | 8 | 32 | 13 |
| 10 years 1 day to 20 years | 3 | 12 | 4 |
| **Recidivism** | | | |
| First incarceration | 12 | 48 | 53 |
| Second or third | 9 | 36 | n.a. |
| Four or more | 4 | 16 | n.a. |
| **Offenses** | | | |
| Crimes of violence | 6 | 24 | 20 |
| Crimes of property | 7 | 28 | 24 |
| Drug-related crimes | 7 | 28 | 16 |
| Public order crimes | 5 | 20 | 40 |
| Involvement with child welfare | 11 | 44 | 50 |
| **Number of children ever born (N = 77)** | | | |
| One | 3 | 12 | 37 |
| Two | 7 | 28 | 30 |
| Three or four | 11 | 44 | 27 |
| Five or more | 4 | 16 | 6 |
| **Ages of children still in mother's custody (N = 57)** | | | |
| less than 1 year | 3 | 5 | n.a. |
| 1 year to 3 years | 5 | 8 | n.a. |
| 3 years to 6 years | 12 | 21 | n.a. |
| 6 years to 10 years | 15 | 21 | n.a. |
| 10 years to 16 years | 15 | 26 | n.a. |
| 16 years to 21 years | 7 | 12 | n.a. |
| **Living with mother prior to incarceration** | | | |
| | 18 | 75 | 72 |

decisions about where children will live upon the imprisonment of their parents usually fall to the mother. However, the challenges of arranging child care differed significantly within the population. For women who were serving a lengthy sentence, defined here as longer than one year, child-care arrangements were more complicated than they were for women serving a briefer term. Mothers who were living alone with their children and were their sole providers had to find their children new places to live. This challenge is different from that posed to women who shared child care with others prior to incarceration and had resources that could be tapped to maintain children in the same living arrangements upon their imprisonment.

On the other hand, if women were not caring for children before incarceration, imprisonment typically did not entail a change in where children lived (Johnston 1995a). Indeed, for some caretakers and children, imprisonment of a family member was a relief. As a result of the incarceration of his or her mother, a child's living arrangement might be more stable; among other things, caretakers might be relieved of the need to "police" and accommodate the woman's behavior while she is on the street. The character of these living arrangements— whether caretakers were supportive, hostile, incompetent, or other— had significant effects on where children lived and how these relationships among the caretakers, the children, and the inmate mothers played out. Finally, the ages of children who required care had to be considered in making child-care arrangements. Some placements that may have been acceptable for young children were not appropriate for teenage girls. While a boyfriend may have been a suitable provider for a teenage son, mothers were less comfortable about a sexual partner's care of a teenage girl. While some families were able to provide care for school-age children, infant care was impossible if adults were working.

Finding places for children to live presents a real challenge for most women coming to prison. Earlier reports on incarcerated females found that 75 percent of the population was living with or responsible for the care of their children prior to sentencing to prison (Johnston 1995a; Snell 1994). This was the case for this sample as well. Among the potential places where children live when their mothers are in prison include with grandparents, siblings, other relations and kin, husbands, boyfriends, friends, foster parents, and others. Although this seems to be a wide array of options, the resources that are actually available to individual women for placing children are quite limited. The fact that patterns of placement differ across race and ethnicity indicates that these options are not equally open to all women; race, ethnicity, and other factors seem to create and constrain the availability of living arrangements.

A number of variables affect the range and type of resources that were available to inmate mothers. How families understood what family members were obliged to do under certain circumstances determined if help would be forthcoming from relatives and kin. How families perceived the event of incarceration determined, in some cases, whether the family would provide care for children. If inmate mothers viewed their families negatively, they were more likely to rely on nonfamily placements, like foster care, husbands and others. These expectations of what families were obliged to do and under what circumstances differed across race and ethnic categories and presented different challenges for white women and women of color in relating to families (Collins 1994; Glenn 1994).

As noted above, patterns of placement varied for children of white, African American, and Hispanic inmate mothers. Where children would live was determined by the combination of available family resources and a woman's assessment of the ability of those caretakers to provide good care for her children. In some instances, the involvement of the child-welfare agency was also a factor. For some women, there were several alternatives from which to select care for children while for other women, there were few. Because of a bad personal experience—for example, being abused or mistreated in foster care herself—some options that might appear viable were, in fact, not an option that a woman would consider. Other options were not workable because of the obligations that might arise by virtue of asking for help, be it from the agency, a family member, an in-law, or other. As Bresler and Lewis (1986) reported, African American inmates were able to identify a wider and larger network of individuals who could be called on for assistance than were white women. While white women appeared more open to using foster care, African American women appeared to avoid foster care as long as family resources could be located.

Children of these inmate mothers lived in a variety of settings.

(See table 4.) Most (46 percent) were in the care of grandparents. The next most prevalent placement was with husbands (28 percent). The third most likely placement was with other relatives (18 percent); the least used placement was foster care (10 percent). Children of two of the women in the sample were living in separate relative households. This breakdown was similar to what Snell (1994) reported in the nationwide survey of living arrangements for children of female inmates.

*Table 4. Placements Used by Inmate Mothers by Race and Ethnicity*

| Race | Grandparent | Foster | Husband | Other Relative | Total |
|------|-------------|--------|---------|----------------|-------|
| White | 4 | 1 | 5 | — | 10 |
| African American | 7 | 2 | — | 5 | 14 |
| Hispanic | 2 | — | 2 | — | 4 |
| Native American | — | — | 1 | — | 1 |
| Total | 13 | 3 | 8 | 5 | 29 |

Accounting for these differences in placement entails examination of several factors. Much of the literature on female offenders has pointed to the link between family and paths to prison (Daly 1994; Miller 1988). Typically, positive relationships with family members prior to imprisonment set the stage for their assistance with children while women were incarcerated. Correspondingly, a woman's estrangement from her family made reliance upon relatives for child care during her incarceration quite unlikely. The quality and character of these relationships, which for the most part preceded incarceration, had important effects on where the children lived while their mothers were in prison. Relationships with family members were not only important during incarceration. Research shows that these relationships have played an important role in determining how women came to be imprisoned in the first place.

PATHS TO PRISON

*White women.* Some research indicates that the ways in which women become involved in street crime differ for white, African American, and Hispanic women. In her study of female hustlers, Miller (1986) identified three "paths to prison." The most typical route to street crime for white women was the "runaway" path. For four inmate mothers in this study, this was path followed. These women grew up in homes they found difficult and fled as soon as they were able to, often becoming involved in drugs and crime through the influence of a boyfriend or male partner. Women described their homes as lower-class or middle-class, and characterized their parents as abusive. Holly, a white woman, described abuse at the hands of her father:

> When I was young my father used to beat the hell out of me. My teachers wanted me to go to the police station to report him but I couldn't do that to him. But I did leave home. I put my mother and father through hell. I got black kids and everything—black men, drugs, no responsibility, no nothing, welfare all my life.

Lonnie, a woman with a brief history of incarceration, noted that her parents were alcohol dependent and that much of her childhood was spent in foster care. Sexual abuse was also part of her history.

> My parents were really bad alcoholics. I spent most of my childhood in foster care. I got molested by one of my uncles and nobody wanted to hear about it.

The role of boyfriends in introducing women to hard drugs has been reported by researchers and was echoed by Nicole.

> I had a boyfriend who got me into heroin. That started me on the streets. Then I got here. That's how I got here. Most of the time it's the boyfriend who gets the woman hooked on drugs. That's a lot of it, believe me. People don't wake up one day and say, "I guess today I'll become a heroin addict." It is his fault. I can put the blame on him. He's the first one who said, "Come on, try this." And I liked it ever since.

The children of these women were in foster care, and some children had been adopted. Most had lost contact with their families. For these inmates, relying on family members—whether these were parents, siblings, or other relatives—for child care did not appear to be an option at all.

Other white women in the study took different paths to prison. Three of the white women were serving their first sentences and their crimes did not reflect the sorts of offenses Miller (1986) noted in her work. Middle- and working-class, these women were not hustlers and had very limited experience on the "street." One woman, convicted for bringing drugs into a correctional facility, characterized her life as "completely normal" except for her involvement in a serious drug trafficking offense and her subsequent incarceration. This woman had been employed full-time at a good job, was married, had an infant, and had little knowledge of the kind of street crimes, like prostitution and hustling, that led so many of the other inmates to prison. Another white woman, convicted of felony shoplifting, was also married and had sons six and seventeen years old. This woman, also conventionally middle-class, had limited exposure to street crime and little knowledge of the lifestyles that characterized the majority of other prisoners. The children of both of these women were living with their husbands, who were both supportive caretakers. It is important to note here that conjugal support provided the bulk of support these women received. Other family members knew about the incarceration, but in neither instance was there a consideration of relying on family members for support other than husbands.

The most atypical group of white women were those who gained access to the streets, crime, and drugs through family members, typically their mothers. Mothers of these three women were drug addicts and prostitutes, and were also involved with child-welfare, mental-health, and criminal justice agencies. April, a white woman who had extensive experience in the criminal justice and substance-abuse systems, explained the involvement of her family in crime and drugs as follows:

> Well, one thing I can say about my mother is that she's forty-five years old and she's been on the street since she's sixteen. She got married and she had a baby. My father beat her, beat her. She got into drugs real bad. She OD'd [overdosed] a few times and came back. My mother had a hard life and I went through all that with her because I was her first baby. She was sixteen when I was born and my father was eighteen. I had to watch her go through a lot of stuff. When I was thirteen, I was cleaning, I was washing, cooking, and

watching my brothers—everything. I raised my brothers for five months when she was a bad drug addict.

Another white woman had a lifelong involvement with the child-welfare agency because of her mother's serious substance-abuse problems.

*Beth:* When I was growing up, my mother was a junkie. Child welfare has always been in my life. I ran away when I was sixteen and spent time at the youth training school. I was put in High View [a school for emotionally disturbed children] and I hated that. The staff was awful. I ran away and they caught me and put me in the training school again. I ran from there. No one could keep me. My mom got a seven-year civil commitment to detox and had to complete the program to keep her kids or she could lose us for good. My mom did real good with the civil commitment but then she relapsed. Then when my baby was born, she got straight for good. I am the spitting image of my mom. We are so much alike in every way.

The children of these inmates were living with their grandmothers. In these families, there was no estrangement that followed the woman's entry into life on the streets, such as that for women like Holly and those profiled in Miller's (1986) research. This generational and family involvement in crime and substance abuse is important to consider when we try to understand if and how families responded to women in these sorts of crises. Family elasticity (the willingness and ability of families to extend help) may be related to the family's expectations of trouble—that members of the family will come into conflict with authorities, be they the schools, the police, courts, employers, or others. Given the prospect that they will, families are prepared to deal with these engagements, not so much as episodes that threaten the family and its status, but as events to be managed. As Farber (1964) noted, not all events are crises. The salient point for family response to crisis is whether family members define the event as one to which they must respond. What for some families is a tragedy—for instance, the incarceration of a young female member on drug or prostitution charges—is a relatively routine event for other families. The variation among family responses to inmate mothers can be attributed to how

family members and women see the incarceration event, their assignment of fault and blame, and their assessments of whether responding to the event will damage the family unit.

*African American women.* In Miller's (1986) study, black women's
routes to prison took several paths, the most likely involving entry
into crime through family members and domestic networks. While
families raising young girls attempted to supervise them and control
their entry to criminal activity, the girls found a variety of opportunities to access the streets. In this sample, seven black women followed
the domestic recruitment path. In some cases, relatives and caretakers introduced women to drug use, as in Tee's case.

> I got into drugs because my aunt used to do it. I used to take her to
> cop [buy drugs] and I always used to say to her, "Why don't you
> leave that stuff alone? You're gonna be a junkie."

In the case of Bernice, a black woman, a caretaker was directly involved with recruitment to life on the streets.

> When I was eight years old, my grandmother took me and all my girl
> cousins and turned us out on the streets. We were all turning tricks.
> When I was thirteen, I called the cops and they got child welfare
> and they grabbed us away and put us all into foster homes.

Children of women who followed this path were living in a variety of placements, predominately relative care. As Lee, a black woman,
noted, families have established a network of arrangements for child care.

> My kids are taken care of between my stepmother and my uncle
> and my brother. Everyone works, so they end up putting them in
> day care and when one gets off work, they pick them up. I know it's
> a lot of hard work for them because they have their priorities and
> stuff. It's kind of hard on them.

A network of support means that children are shared and no caretaker
is singularly burdened with child care. As Tee stated, responsibility
for children is distributed among family members.

> My niece takes care of my children, but she has a lot of help. My
> sister has one of my kids, and my other sister has one. My brother
> has the boy, so they are kind of split up. I have a really good family.

For other women, family resources were depleted, forcing the use
of foster care. Potential caretakers were already overwhelmed with
demands from other family members. In other instances, the family
had been deemed unacceptable as an appropriate home by the child-
welfare authorities. Finally, prospective family caretakers were saddled
with their own problems, like serious illness or alcohol or drug abuse,
and were temporarily unavailable to care for children. In explaining
why families were not caring for their children, women maintained
that the families were willing but were unable to help at the time
assistance was needed. Bernice's family of origin had a long record
with child welfare, and was excluded by the authorities as a suitable
place for children to live.

> My kids were going to live with my mother, maybe, but she had a
> record with child welfare and they pulled those kids out of her house.
> There was nobody else around.

Because of difficulties in her family, Margaret, an inmate who had
been incarcerated many times over a ten-year period, had no alternatives but foster care to place her children.

> When I started coming here, my mother had a drinking problem so
> we had to give them up [that is, place the children in the care of the
> state].

In two cases where family resources were depleted because of
criminal and drug involvement of other family members, children were
placed in foster care and eventually were adopted. One woman had
lost custody of her seven children to the state following the long-term
involvement of child welfare in her family. In some cases, child welfare intervened because children were born drug-exposed or because
a complaint of abuse or neglect had been substantiated by the agency.
Opening a case with child welfare meant that the family would remain
under the agency's inspection, with associated case plans, appearances

in family court, and the threat of loss of custody and termination of parental rights. Although Bernice stated that she was not taking drugs during pregnancy, the child-welfare department took the child into custody. She reported that the involvement of child welfare was nearly impossible to terminate.

> I feel like I'm having babies for the state. Once child welfare gets in your life, they're always there. They stick with you forever.

The entry of child welfare into a family's life makes it difficult for some women to balance their needs to manage child care and children and to accommodate the demands of child welfare. Regaining children from foster care requires careful management of workers and a clear demonstration of fitness as mother. Strategies for demonstrating fitness will be discussed in a later chapter.

Less typically, black women gained access to street crime and drugs as young adults. This was the case for three women in the sample. They described themselves as good students and as the only renegades in churchgoing families; they were lured into street crime and drugs by peers and boyfriends, not by family members. Although being the "black sheep" may have reflected social distance in white families, resulting in estrangement, being the only individual with serious drug and criminal involvement in these African American families appeared to increase chances that family resources were available for child placement. Black families in this study were more elastic, it appears, even when girls were the only deviant in the family. Extending help to a criminal female family member did not seem to carry the threat to status that it did for families of white inmate mothers. Maya, an inmate mother without prior incarcerations, put the onus of her involvement in crime and drugs clearly on herself and did not attribute it to family members.

> I had a father and I had a mother. I had love. My mother and father don't smoke or drink or do drugs. So I come from good home. I just went the wrong way completely. I turned to coke. My oldest sister that has my daughter, she doesn't do drugs. One of my other older sisters, she doesn't do drugs. She just drinks. She's not an alcoholic and then my baby sister, she doesn't do nothing neither. It's just me. I went in a completely different direction.

The onset of drug use and the "fast life" at early adulthood sometimes happened despite attempts by caretakers to provide children
with good homes. Belinda, for instance, placed no blame on her parents because of their inability to keep her away from the streets:

> I come from a good family. I have one parent and I wasn't abused or
> anything like that. I was an A student in school, Homecoming Queen,
> best personality, best dressed. It's not like that. Our parents did all
> they could for us and then they had to let us go at a certain age. I got
> introduced to drugs. I liked it and the fast life. My mother did the
> best and everything she could.

Families of African American women appeared to extend help with
respect to child care during incarceration as long as resources were
available. Because the resources of some families were so exhausted,
foster care had to be utilized by inmate mothers. Black inmate mothers whose families were conventional were able to rely on family members for child care in a way that was not available for white inmate
mothers; however, white inmates did have access to husbands, a resource
that was not identified by African American women in this study. This
is not to say that men were not involved in child care in African American families; they were simply not identified as primary caregivers.

*Hispanic women.* Hispanic women's paths to prison are facilitated
by involvement with drugs, according to Miller (1986). The four
women in this study somewhat fit this profile. Two women, foreign-
born and recent immigrants, were serving long sentences for drug trafficking and had no prior involvement in the criminal justice system or
substance abuse agencies. Rosa characterized her parents as conventional and hardworking. She is serving a five-year sentence for drug
delivery. Her children are living with her parents.

> It's weird, too, you know. I got into all this because I was with the
> wrong person. My mother and my father always worked. They even
> worked on holidays for overtime. And you know I didn't want to do
> that [work so hard]. I wanted an easy way to get money. My mother
> she was saying to me, "Why are you doing this? You didn't see this
> from us."

Two other Hispanic women, born in this country, were drug users and involved in a series of minor property crimes. Their routes to prison were the domestic and runaway paths identified by Miller (1986). Yvonne, serving an eighteen-month sentence for shoplifting, had been to prison on several occasions. The involvement of her parents in drugs eased her entry into serious drug use.

> My parents are both heroin addicts—functional addicts. My dad just got into treatment and he's like fifty years old. I started with drugs because I saw everybody around me doing it. My friends, my cousins, my sister, I would watch all this. I wanted what they had. I wanted to hang out, be wanted, be grown up. One thing led to another, snorting cocaine, smoking pot, sniffing dope.

The children of Yvonne were living with her husband. Hispanic women were using a variety of placements for their children. Hispanic women were like white women in that they placed children with husbands. Because they were able to rely on family members for care of their children, their patterns of placement resembled that of African American women as well.

*Summary.* Paths to prison are, in part, a result of relationships with families and these influence where children live while their mothers are incarcerated. Some women gain access to criminal lifestyles through families, while, for others, families provide some insulation from the attractions of the street. In most cases, inmate mothers have some say in where children live. In assessing caretaking options, inmate mothers examine the viability of providers and evaluate how family and others would provide care for their children. The appeal and availability of family providers are determined by women's attributions of blame for their own paths to prison. How women understand and define their course to imprisonment is a major factor in how they judge whether their family represents a good place for their children to live while they are incarcerated.

ATTRIBUTIONS FOR IMPRISONMENT

*White women.* Differences in living arrangements for children could also be linked to differences among women in their attributions of how they came to be incarcerated. Some white women linked their lives on the street and their coming to prison to bad homes, poor parenting and inadequate supervision and protection by their mothers and fathers. For white women, a negative assessment of their own child rearing pushed them away from seriously considering the home of their parents for the care of their children. In these cases, husbands or partners were good options for placement. For other white women whose parents were involved in crime, drugs, and life on the streets earlier in their lifetimes, children were readily placed with their grandmothers, as many of these older caretakers had retreated from life on the streets and addiction. In addition, grandparents' experiences in the criminal and addict lifestyle made these families more elastic in terms of being willing to respond to the needs of these younger family members with similar problems.

*African American women.* Black women seldom connected their involvement in crimes and drugs to bad parenting. They maintained that their mothers and other caretakers did the best they could in child rearing but that the temptations of the street were too much for them to resist. For most African American women, the network of relatives and kin provided enough space within which to find a place for children to stay. For white women, this circle of available help was smaller and more constrained. This wider network of support for black women seldom carried the negative assessment of caretakers that characterized the evaluations by white women.

*Hispanic women.* Typically, Hispanic women's attributions of paths to prison were connected to the lure of quick money through drug sales. Most did not trace their involvement in crime to family and poor upbringing. These women typically relied on family members for child care. However, in one instance, a Hispanic inmate mother whose parents were still active drug addicts traced her dependence on drugs and accompanying criminality to her parents. This Hispanic woman relied on her husband and had little involvement with her family while she was in prison.

OPTIONS FOR CHILD PLACEMENT

As women confronted the challenge of placing children in someone else's care, they weighed the value and viability of different placement resources. These differed in some respects by race and ethnicity. Husbands appeared to be more available as resources for white and Hispanic women; foster care appeared to be more of an option for white women; and family resources appeared to be more extensive for African American women and for Hispanic women.

*Husbands.* According to national data, husbands provide about 25 percent of the care for inmate children (Snell 1994). This is somewhat greater than that reported by other studies, which estimate this figure to be as low as 8 percent (Henriques 1982) and as high as 22 percent (Stanton 1980). In the present sample, husbands appeared to be more available as caretakers for white and Hispanic children than they were for African American children. Eight husbands in this sample were providing care for children. Most husbands assumed care by default. Four were living with the mother and the children prior to incarceration, and few of the white mothers relied on relatives other than the husbands to handle child care. Meredith, a white woman serving a four-year sentence for drug trafficking, suggested that both she and her husband were estranged from their families and neither could rely on family for child care. "I really don't have any family and neither does my husband. It's just him and me."

Marcia contended that either the child's mother or father must be the primary caretaker, and that others would not be adequate for the task. "I can't imagine anyone but my husband taking care of my baby. If it wasn't me, it had to be him."

In some cases, inmate mothers reported that not only were husbands a good substitute, they were better caretakers than themselves and that the children were more attached to their fathers. Yvonne remarked, "That's one thing. I would never separate them from their dad, because they really love him. They love me, too, but you know they are really crazy about him."

For some women, fathers were not involved with their children as caretakers until the mother's imprisonment. In four cases, the mother and father were estranged prior to incarceration, and this continued during the imprisonment. As the legal and biological parent of the child, fathers had claims to children and, in some cases, were working to gain custody of the children and to separate them legally from the mother. Placement with the father was often not the choice of the mother, but one that arose due to her inability to prevent his taking possession of the children at the time she was incarcerated. Active challenges to the mother's custody of her children were mounted by white and Hispanic fathers.

*Foster care.* Nationally, foster homes provide about 9 percent of the care for children of women in prison (Snell 1994). This figure varies in research reports from 7.3 percent (Bloom and Steinhart 1993) to a high of 26.3 percent (Johnston 1995b). Although for some women foster care was the worst possible placement for children, for others it was the best of all alternatives. The viability of foster care as an option was compared to the use of one's family and/or boyfriend or husband. White women appeared to be more likely to use foster care as a good and desirable placement option for children. This was reflected in conversations with two white women enrolled in the parenting program but not included in the sample interviewed in this research. These inmate mothers had children in foster care and both evaluated the care their children were receiving as good or excellent. In both instances, involvement with child welfare was voluntary. White women may have felt that they could better manage the child-welfare system and its caseworkers, although all women spoke about the importance of getting the right social worker assigned to a case. Stacy noted the paradoxical nature of contacting child welfare for help, suggesting that asking for assistance meant that child welfare would initiate an investigation into parental fitness.

> There is a problem with the [child-welfare] system. It seems like when you really need help the only way you can get it is for somebody to make sure that you done something wrong.

The evaluation by women that getting help from the child-welfare system also meant becoming identified as a case under investigation resulted in several women avoiding contact with the agency. This had the effect of children remaining in questionable situations because the inmate feared the consequences of bringing the matter to the attention of the agency, especially while she was in prison.

As noted previously, black inmate mothers made minimal use of foster care. This lack of use did not appear to be result of denial of services on the part of the child-welfare agency; it appeared more likely that African American mothers did not trust that the agency would provide good, safe care for black children. Typically, foster care was considered to be the worst of all possible options by African American inmate mothers. Maya, serving an eight-year sentence for manslaughter, noted that someone in her family would come forward to provide care and that resistance to foster care would be mounted by the entire family. "They [my family] would never put my daughter in foster care. Somebody would come to take care of her."

Other black women suggested reasons why foster care was avoided by black families.

> *Paulette:* Those foster parents don't know nothing about black people. My girl was in foster care once and they really messed up her hair. She came home with it all cut up.

Alice, speaking directly about her concerns about African American children in white foster homes, worried that children were in danger, specifically from child molestation.

> Seems like all the time you hear about something happening to somebody's kid in foster care. A lot of molestation happens in these white homes. It happened to my friend's kids.

Despite this strong distaste for foster care, women with repeated involvement in crime and drugs were in relatively powerless positions with respect to the child-welfare agency. In these instances, foster care was utilized when the child-welfare agency was already involved with the family and viewed the family setting as potentially damaging to the children. In some families, resources to deal with the crisis of where children should live had been strained by the severe economic stress, drug involvement, or criminal activity of other family members. Families have virtually no power to resist foster care of their children. In some instances, family members who were not drug and crime involved may have been overwhelmed by the needs of the rest of the family and pseudofamily members.

*Family.* Family resources for caring for children includes grandparents, siblings, aunts, cousins, and in-laws. Snell (1994) reports that family care represents 71 percent of all placements. For black women, this represents 80 percent of placements; for Hispanic women, 77 percent; and for white women, 55 percent. For some families, the incarceration event was one that brought shame on the family, as well as disgracing the individual. Efforts to maintain status in the community may have militated against some families helping the woman inmate and her children. This sentiment was conveyed by Holly.

> I was the only one in my family who went wrong. They don't want to hear nothing from me. My parents are hardworking people and nobody likes my lifestyle or the way I choose to live my life. When I called them up to tell them that I gave birth to twins, they just hung up the phone.

Holly's estrangement from her family predated her imprisonment. Typically, women like Holly suggested that their families would find their current imprisonment unacceptable and that asking for or receiving assistance from family members was out of the question. In some instances, women reported that they would not go to their families for help because these homes would not be good places for their children to live. White women also accounted for the noninvolvement of their families in the care of the children by suggesting that their use of relative caretakers would tie them to obligations and debts that they could not repay. Holly pointed to significant status differences between herself and her family.

> My other sister is married with twins and another boy. They just built a house. Her husband owns a company. My brother followed in my father's tracks and works with an insurance company. He just got married and had a baby. He loves his wife and the baby. My other sister works at a department store, worked there all her life. If I put my kids with them, I would never hear the end of it. Every time there was a holiday or something, they would throw it up in my face, how they helped when I was in jail. I would rather take my chances with foster care.

These differences between the inmate mother and her siblings made her going to them for assistance an unlikely proposition. Being a family member in need did not guarantee that significant family resources would be available, even if others had resources that might be shared. Some white women contended that foster care was a better alternative because, unlike family obligations, one could terminate involvement with the child-welfare agency when the case was completed. This was contrasted with family debts that white women believed would be unpaid despite the work they would be doing as mothers after incarceration. In other words, relying on family members for child care under these conditions would tie these inmate mothers to an unpayable debt.

Additionally, white women argued that their parents had completed child-rearing obligations by raising them. Expectations that the grandparents would reengage child-care work under these circumstances were not ones they could imagine or suggest to their parents. Holly and Irene, white women with multiple incarcerations, explained the limited involvement of their mothers in taking care of their children.

> *Holly:* My mother said to me, "If I take care of your kids, it will be when I want to and if I want to. Nobody but me took care of you kids when you were growing up and nobody but you should be bringing up your kids."

> *Irene:* My mother already raised her kids. Why should she have to take the responsibility for mine?

Even when parents of white inmate mothers came forward to provide care, this gesture was characterized as a payment in kind for the child minding that the inmate mother did when she was a child or as issuing out of guilt for some defect in the caregiver's parenting.

> *April:* She took my kids because she felt so guilty about the way she raised me. This is like a payback.

> *Beth:* My mother took my kid when she was born. All of a sudden she got straight and sober and started preaching to me about stuff.

For white women, caretaking by parents seemed to issue more out of obligation than out of generosity or out of expected family work. In some instances, the parents of white inmate mothers did not provide child care until it was determined that the only alternative was foster care. On the other hand, none of the black or Hispanic women in this sample suggested that their parents or kin were taking care of children out of obligation or that grandparents had completed their careers as child keepers. These caregivers were characterized as available for child care; they were ready to provide support to inmate mothers and prepared to assume financial support for children. Family for black and Hispanic women included multiple members who were involved with their children and assisted the primary caretaker. As Belinda, an African American woman serving her second sentence, explained, getting care for her children when she was involved with drugs was not an issue.

> For black people and our generation, there would be a long-distance relative from East Chipopee who would come to take care of one kid. When I was in the world using drugs, everybody would say, "If you're not ready to take care of your kids, I'll take them till you're ready." That problem I didn't have.

Vanessa, another black woman, described the ready involvement of her mother in child keeping.

> My mother has been taking care of my kids. She's a saint that way. I have no plans to follow in her footsteps but I thank God she is there and ready to take care of them whenever.

This sentiment was echoed by a Hispanic woman, Rosa.

> My family is always there for me. My mother and father are right there. Anything I need I have and that goes for my kids, too.

*Summary.* Women in this study voiced differing cultural expectations about what family would provide in times of crisis. For the most part, black and Hispanic families appeared more likely to extend support to take care of children than did white families. White inmate mothers' expectations about family responsiveness were more constrained, with obligations more clearly and carefully demarcated and measured out in terms of fair exchange. Reliance upon foster care appeared more likely for children of inmate mothers when the family could not provide (in the case of black children) or when inmate mothers felt foster care was a better alternative than family care (in the case of white mothers).

INMATE MOTHERS THEORIZE ABOUT RACE AND ETHNICITY

These differences in where children of white, Hispanic, and African American women lived were described by the inmate mothers themselves and were explained by their relying upon what they knew about racial and ethnic family structures and differences in responses to family crises. Explaining the differences among white, black, and Hispanic families, Yvonne, a Hispanic woman, observed,

> In black families, there is more of a bond and I think they mistrust white people to take care of their kids. The child welfare is the white man's system so the white women don't mind using it as much as black and Spanish girls do. Spanish families are right in between. It's not that we don't have a bond but that our families are so strict that they're hard to deal with.

Another Hispanic woman, comparing white and Latino families, explained that help from white families is conditional and limited.

> In [white] American families, when you are eighteen they kick you out of the house and you are on your own. But in Spanish families, your family is there—100 percent of the time. They are always there for you.

Almost all respondents reported that black families had more of a "bond," a deeper family commitment, and were able to get through family crises better than white families. One black woman suggested that white families had high expectations for their children and did not expect their girls to get into trouble.

> *Tee:* For white families, they don't expect that they will get jammed up [in trouble with the criminal justice system]. If a white girl messes up, she brings shame on the whole family. White families have real short fuses. You mess up and you are out. Black families aren't like that.

White women also noted that white families were different from families of color, arguing that this was the result of white family members being "out for themselves" and not willing to help members in trouble. But interestingly, despite the fact that the family was not a viable placement option for these white women, many understood the situation "as the way things were." The refusal of family to provide care was seen as normative behavior and not unexpected based on their knowledge of what other white families would do if their female family members had gotten into prison and involved with drugs. These understandings of racial and ethnic differences among families and how viable family resources were for inmate mothers in trouble revealed important knowledge by women. These differences played an important role in how women saw themselves as mothers in relationship to their children, to caretakers, and to other mothers.

### CARETAKER MANAGEMENT OF MOTHERS

Because of imprisonment, inmate mothers were no longer in daily contact with children as their primary caretakers. As substitute providers, caretakers exerted enormous influence on children and on their relationships with their mothers. Some caretakers worked to maintain inmate mothers in central positions as mothers vis-à-vis their children, even though inmate mothers were not involved in primary care of the children. In other instances, caretakers moved into mother positions vacated when mothers had left the children with others to pursue crime or drugs. Caretakers in these situations might have moved to replace mothers as primary caretakers on a permanent or a temporary basis. The nature and quality of these relationships will be taken up in the next section.

At the same time that mothers attempted to construct and manage motherhood in prison, interested others also exerted influence on their performance of this role. Caretakers tried to direct the behavior of mothers by issuing ultimatums and negotiating bargains around the care of children. In some instances, caretakers took responsibility for children before being asked for help and assistance. Caretakers often asserted their rights to children when mothers were assumed not to be performing motherhood to the satisfaction of others. Serious use of drugs appears to be a behavior that brings the mother's ability to care for children to the attention of family members. As Luisa explained, some families intervened in a mother's caretaking of children if they found the mother was not providing for children in a way that met their standards.

> I could have had drugs whenever I wanted them. But my mother said she would take my kids if I did drugs. I could go ahead and do drugs, but she would take the kids. I had no choice—drugs or my kids. I took my kids and I been clean five years.

Caretakers were also in a difficult position with respect to mothers and their children. Balancing caretaking with trying to exert influence over the mother's behavior put them in the position of issuing ultimatums and then backing off from them for the sake of the children in their care, as Vanessa explained.

> I will go live with my mom after my release. She makes it so easy. I don't have to think about money or the kids, so I can spend my money on something else. My mom gets real hard-core sometimes. Sometimes she says, "If you don't straighten up, you're going to get out of this house. But your kids stay here." And then other times she says, "You and your kids gotta get out of here," and I say, "Oh sure, Mom," but I know she don't mean it.

Cynthia indicated how family members negotiated caretaking obligations and how these changed and were made contingent upon her changing her behavior.

> My mother always had my kids. Well, then my mother died, my sister jumped in to help. But she wouldn't let me go [to run the streets] like my mother did. Your sister is not your mother. My sister made it clear that I couldn't do this thing for the rest of my life. When I was on my missions [looking for drugs and getting high], my sister watched the kids, but now she won't help unless she thinks I'm trying to do something different.

Although caretakers endeavored to exert some control over mothers by pushing them to assume responsibility for children, their power was compromised by virtue of their attachment to and concern for children. This caretaking of children may have been temporary or long-term. Although incarceration was disruptive for most inmate mothers and their families, for some repeat offenders the mechanisms to take care of children in the mother's absence were well established. Repeated sentences to prison made incarceration a routine event in which older children and relatives assumed ongoing responsibility for the management of the household. Inez had served thirteen terms over a twenty-year period. Patterns of child keeping while she was incarcerated were well established.

> I been in and out of here so many times since 1985 that someone else always takes care of them when I come here.

However, even in instances where these arrangements were routine, a mother's return to the community could disrupt the family unit and be a disorienting event for the caretaker and the children. As Inez explained, as others take care of children over long periods of time, they may assume they are in control and seek to exert ownership of the children.

> Every time I come home, my kids run to me. My mother gets so attached to them that she gets mad when I come home. One time she called child welfare and said that my kids had run away.

Much of the permanent substitute care that was arranged for children was done informally, outside the realm of child welfare. Mothers and caretakers negotiated obligations, expectations, and rights to children, setting down rules for visitation and discipline. Some of these arrangements paralleled those found in child welfare, with graduated engagement by caretakers in children's lives as mothers reduced their involvement with the children or failed to perform up to the standards set by the caregiver.

In the case of a white woman who had given birth at eighteen, an agreement was signed and notarized by the inmate's mother and herself, rendering care of the child to the grandmother. The inmate mother visited the home daily, lived in a separate household, and maintained a drug habit and criminal lifestyle. The situation never came to the attention of the child-welfare agency. Such families provided structured arrangements to manage mothers' relationships with their children and attempted to intervene in informal ways to protect grandchildren and control mothers' behaviors.

When these informal arrangements began to fail or when caretakers could no longer control a mother's behavior, they enlisted the help of child-welfare authorities. Contacting child welfare provided some relief for the caretaker. However, it also sometimes meant the eventual loss of the child to child-welfare system if there were no viable caretakers at hand. In two cases, husbands of drug-using women called child welfare for assistance. While this meant that the family had to negotiate custody with child welfare and abide by agency plans and mandates, the intervention of the agency provided male caretakers with some leverage to control the behavior of their wives.*

ASSESSING CARETAKERS

When women are facing incarceration, a "good mother" becomes one who can find and secure safe and predictable care for her children. Several women remarked that they could have served extensive time in prison if they were assured that children were well taken care of. This indicates that mothers believed that other caretakers might have been adequate to the task of raising children and that they were not the only individuals uniquely qualified to raise and take care of their children.

The type of arrangement—whether it was a family-based setting, a conjugally based placement, or foster care—by no means predicted the character or quality of the relationship with the care provider. As noted above, inmate mothers carefully assessed the quality and motivations of caretakers. Mothers characterized caretakers as overwhelmed, supportive, competent, or hostile. Because of other family work and responsibilities, caretakers may have been exhausted by the demands of child care. Caretakers may support the mother during incarceration with the hope of restoring her to her place as the mother of her children (that is, as caretaker) upon release. In other cases, caregivers were hostile to the mother and conveyed negative messages, antagonistic attitudes, and false information about the mother to her children (Johnston 1995a).

---

*Relying on state and voluntary agencies to address problems with children, parents, and spouses has been documented by Gordon (1988). In *Heroes of Their Own Lives*, she documents how intervention by social agencies was often provoked by members of families who sought to exercise some authority over family members whose behavior was beyond their control.

*Caretaker fatigue.* Caretakers who had provided child care for long periods of time were described as exhausted by inmate mothers. Inez described the fatigue and exhaustion of her mother, who had provided care for her six children (ranging in age from five to twenty-one years of age) over a twenty-year period.

> I can't keep coming here, because my mom is so old. I know she can only take so much, and she's tired of me. She says everyday, "I'm so tired of you. You're always in there [prison]. You're never out here with us." And that is true.

Some of these caretakers were ill and unable to continue providing care for extended periods of time. Irene characterized her elderly parents as unable to care any longer for her son. A hyperactive twelve-year-old, Irene's son was beyond the ability of her parents to manage, resulting in their issuing an ultimatum to her.

> My parents are old now and they're sick. They say to me, "You come home and get into trouble and we will put Dan with the state because we can't do it anymore."

Neither of these inmate mothers had ever provided full-time care of their children, and both were running out of caretaker indulgence. Despite the fact that they had not occupied a central role with respect to child care, both demonstrated good knowledge of their children and the challenges their children presented to caretakers. Other women with limited roles in the lives of their children knew fewer details about children and were less able to identify particular problems faced and presented by their children.

*Caretakers as incompetent.* In other instances, inmate mothers believed that caretakers were incompetent and incapable of providing good child care. These inmate mothers alleged that caretakers were involved with drugs, allowing children too much freedom, and not performing up to the mother's standards. Mothers, in these situations, were afforded few good options. Because they knew these caretakers and had relationships with them prior to incarceration, they were able to exert some influence on their behavior. They attempted to contact a mutual friend or a relative to bring some pressure on the caretakers.

If this failed, addressing the problem meant contacting the child-welfare agency to file a complaint. This would bring the situation to the attention of child welfare, possibly for the first time, and potentially put the mother's status with respect to the child in some jeopardy, because she was incarcerated. Stacy, the mother of a four-year-old boy, worried about her husband's care of her children.

> Their father is taking drugs. I don't like the way he takes care of the kids. When my son comes [to visit] he tells me about things. My mother says stuff, too. But I can't call child welfare, because they would grab my son and I could lose everything.

Because there were no other viable caretakers, contacting child welfare could result in the child's removal to foster care and the opening of an investigation about the mother's fitness as a parent. Depending on the length of her sentence and the jurisdiction in which she lives, incarceration could initiate action by child welfare to terminate her rights to her child.*

Another woman was convinced her husband was using drugs and not providing good care for their children. The children had recently been seriously assaulted by the father's relatives. The mother contacted child welfare to file a complaint of child abuse against her husband. Susan explained the conflict between protecting her children from harm and protecting her legal standing with respect to the children.

> All I expected of him was a few things. He didn't have to do things my way or be like me. All he had to do was pay some attention to

---

*Genty (1995) and others (Barry 1985; Beckerman 1994; Beckerman 1991) have noted the special concerns of inmate mothers with respect to legal action regarding the termination of parental rights. Historically, in some jurisdictions, the mere fact of incarceration served as prima facie evidence of abandonment. Due to important reforms in some states, inmate mothers are now subject to the same challenges that face other mothers who are seeking to avoid termination of parental rights, that is, compliance with state rules and regulations governing permanency planning. However, the ability of inmate mothers to participate in permanency planning efforts geared to reunification with children is hampered by visiting policies in prisons, lack of familiarity of child welfare workers with correctional systems, lack of legal services for inmate mothers, lack of communication with caseworkers, who are burdened with heavy caseloads, and other factors.

them and keep them safe. So I called them [child welfare]. I just hope they don't TPR me [terminate my parental rights].

It is important to note here that some caretakers protected the inmate mother from child welfare's interest in her case. If the agency believed that no caretakers were available for child, then it might have moved to bring the child into foster care.

*Caretakers as supportive and competent.* Fourteen of the women reported that the caretakers of their children were supportive and competent. Support included involving the mother in the decisions made about the child, upholding her role as the child's mother, offering the child a place to live, establishing a relationship that the mother evaluated as superior to that she was providing, and doing things the mother considered important to do with respect to the child. Tee suggested that caretakers supported a mother by assuring her that her children knew her as a key figure in their lives, not just as another adult or other caretaker.

> She made sure my kids knew me. I think families are more likely to do that when they think the mother's interested in getting her kids back.

Inmate mothers also considered caretakers supportive when they performed the routine tasks of mothering. Husbands who took on this work received special praise, as exemplified by Kathy's kudos of her husband.

> He does everything now. He cooks and washes and takes my son to school and shopping. I can't believe he does so much.

In rearing a child, decisions must constantly be made about care, treatment, discipline, and related issues. Having an opportunity to discuss these matters was very important for inmate mothers and one that contributed to the positive evaluation of caretakers. Rose and April expressed satisfaction with their role in decision making regarding their children.

> *Rose:* My mother is always calling me. "What do you think about this? What about that?" I say, "Don't even ask, just do it," because I know it will be right thing.

*April:* Yeah, we discuss that all the time—school, doctors—anything that goes on with my kids, we discuss. I usually agree with her. But she discusses it with me. She won't do nothin' as far as my kids are concerned without me knowin'. My mother makes most of the decisions and I agree with her. I would do the same thing as her, so I let her decide.

Some inmate mothers faced a paradox in assessing the quality of child care. While feeling that their children were receiving good care from providers, they could be very concerned that their children were growing increasingly attached to other caretakers. This raised the question for mothers and caretakers about whether it was possible to provide good care for children without undermining the mother's place (or potential place) in the life of the child. In her research on mothers, nannies, and au pairs, McDonald (1998) contrasted "maximizing" (in which mothers suggested that children benefited from the care provided by others) and "minimizing" (in which mothers contended that the contact with care providers was too brief or that the children were not significantly or importantly attached to substitute care providers). In the following statement, Lonnie typifies a mother who has assigned maximum benefit to the impact of care providers:

He's with foster parents who really love him a lot. They are just great with him. He's very attached to them.

These caretakers were assessed positively because they fulfilled the wishes of the mother for the care of her children. Supportive caretakers were those who shared control of children, who performed important tasks, who kept mothers informed about their children, and who did not threaten or sabotage mothers' relationships with their children.

*Caretakers as hostile.* The quality of the relationship between inmate mothers and caretakers was not always positive. The benefits of supportive relationships became apparent when one compares the situation of inmate mothers with positive caretaker relationships to those of inmate mothers who were dealing with hostile caretakers. Hostile caretakers undermined inmate mothers' roles and positions vis-à-vis their children by limiting contact, contesting custody and ownership, and actively working to exclude or replace the mother in her position as the child's central caretaker. The children of a Hispanic woman serving a very long sentence were taken from the United States back to Central America by her husband shortly after her incarceration. Rachel explained how it was nearly impossible for her to maintain contact with her children.

> Since I came here, my kids can't write to me. I write all these letters, but they won't let them write back. So, I know they know I love them, but it is hard this way.

Meredith's husband had exerted ownership and rights to their child by moving out of state to minimize the inmate mother's contact with her.

> My husband will contest the custody. It will be hard for the parole board to give me parole because my case was so well known. My husband took my daughter to Mississippi to live so we just talk on the phone.

The power of inmate mothers to manage relationships with children was especially compromised if other parties were pursuing adoption or custody of the child, and if the case was active with child welfare. Holly noted the difficulty of maintaining contact with children when others were interested in them. The inmate mother then had to balance her interest in seeing the child against the foster parents' interest in minimizing the child's emotional response to the visit. This was probably upsetting to Holly, but not seeing the child might threaten her claim that she was interested in her son.

> These foster parents really want to adopt Joey. So, every time the worker brings him, the foster parents complain that he comes back all sick and upset, and they try to tell the social worker he was too young to visit. I have an order from the Family Court that says he has to visit and that she has to bring him, so there's nothing they can do about it.

The quality of relationships with caretakers both reflected prior relationships and predicted the course of inmate mother careers.

SUMMARY

The availability of child-care options available to mothers is an artifact of cultural differences among women about what families do and what they are obligated to do for members. It also reflects differences in family structure and their ability and willingness to extend help to other family members in times of need. These ideas about family also affected relationships with the caretakers who worked to support or undermine the mothers' relationships with their children. Because they are in prison, the ability of inmate mothers to parent is under question, and children in this situation may become the objects of battles over their control. These social situations—demonstrating fitness and negotiating ownership of children—are discussed in the next chapter.

# Chapter 4

# Demonstrating Fitness and Negotiating Ownership of Children

As social actors, individuals are constantly called to account for themselves. Their presentations of self are managed effectively if their actions match their claimed identity. As mothers and inmates, inmate mothers are faced with the social situation of demonstrating fitness to be mothers. This display occurs in a correctional environment that constantly can undermine fitness claims by inmate mothers. Inmate mothers are interested in demonstrating fitness because it is usually linked to ownership of children—that is, the rights to raise, manage, and control children, and be involved as a key figure in their lives. Once again, the institutional setting works to weaken an inmate's bargaining power and claims to children with respect to others who may also be making claims. These negotiations over children may be successfully resolved in the favor of an inmate mother, may be partially won, or may result in loss of rights to and "ownership" of children.

## DEMONSTRATING FITNESS

For inmates who are also mothers, one important area of accounting is demonstrating fitness as a mother. Demonstrations of fitness are somewhat constrained by the demands of audiences outside the prison walls and the situational contingencies inside the institution. Establishing fitness as mother also requires successfully claiming mother identity. In our sample this was accomplished by identity talk, by taking up a

75

variety of strategies to make one's actions with respect to motherhood congruent with one's claim to that identity, and by planning for reunification. The symbolic value of this kind of work is important to consider, because these actions are not simply instrumental activities but are endowed with meaning that supports definitions of good mothering (Garey 1995).

IDENTITY TALK

Demonstrating fitness required "identity talk." As Goffman (1963) noted, the mere fact of being in prison poses threats to identity, because others can employ the fact of imprisonment to suggest they know something about the inmate and can impute something about her character.

> In certain circumstances the social identity of those an individual is with can be used as a source of information concerning his own social identity, the assumption being that he is what the others are . . . an analysis of how people manage the information they convey about themselves will have to consider how they deal with the contingencies of being seen "with" particular others. (1963, 48)

Inmate mothers had not only to resist identity as inmates but to resist identification as bad mothers. For inmate mothers, identity development necessarily involved comparing oneself to other mothers. LeFlore and Holston (1989) suggest that a woman inmate's perception of whether she was fulfilling her role as a mother depends on her understanding of what other good mothers do. Hays (1996) suggests a similar mechanism in that women select from among a variety of information sources to develop their own ideas about good mothering.

Through the use of contrastive rhetoric, women attempt to distinguish themselves from other inmates, from their own past selves, and from others in similar situations. As used by Coffey and Atkinson, contrastive rhetoric refers to

> accounts in which the speaker and his or her practices or values are legitimated or justified by means of comparison with what goes on elsewhere, what has been done in the past, or what others do. The contrasts are constructed so as to provide the hearer with the oppor-

tunity to recognize which state of affairs is to be preferred. (1996, 104)

Rhetorical devices were used by inmate mothers to distance, bracket, and defend their identities as mothers.

*Identity as gendered mandates.* Because the women were in prison, they were violating gender mandates about femininity. "Real" women do not go to prison, especially if they have children (Farrell 1998). Normative expectations are that mothers do not risk becoming separated from children as a result of their involvement in illegal activities. Involvement in criminality does not seem to threaten a male's parental status as significantly as it does a female's. As voiced by Nicole, a repeat offender,

> Men can be criminals but mothers should be different. We shouldn't be out of control and a lot of us are.

Reflecting dominant views, inmate mothers recognized that their convict status significantly undermined their claims to motherhood. Motherhood was viewed by inmates as a position that should have isolated a woman from criminality and directed her attention and concern to children.

*Identity as mother damaged by imprisonment.* Women employed a number of devices to distinguish their own positions and performances as inmates from their claims to identities as good mothers. Frequently, women equated the mere fact of imprisonment with the inability to do mothering or to be a mother to one's children. The status of "inmate" called into question a woman's claim to "mother." For some inmates, incarceration placed women out of the mothering role for the term of incarceration. Meredith, a white middle-class woman, argued that one could not be a good mother and an inmate.

> Everyone here is a bad mother simply by the fact that they are not with their kids.

Although parenting programs and extended visiting programs are designed to reinforce the connections between parents and their children,

Marcia suggested that seeing children while in prison was a bitter reminder that their lives were going on despite her imprisonment, and that others were occupying positions as caretakers and decision makers.

> Being an actual parent is not something I see here [in the parenting program]. It's almost a reminder that you're not home anymore. You can't have control of your kids and you can't have an active part in raising them.

These women argued that women in prison could not be mothers simply because they were incarcerated. Mothering in prison was not a real option for these women. An inmate mother can maintain her position as a child's mother by virtue of giving birth, but because she was not with her children, performing as their mother, she cannot claim that she was mothering in prison.

*Identity defended by distancing.* Inmate mothers employed a number of strategies to put distance between themselves and other inmates. These strategies were similar to those employed by the homeless, who invented alternative identities in situations where positive self-identity was under siege (Snow and Anderson 1993). Typically, even though they were in prison, inmate mothers would suggest that they were unlike most inmates. Inmate women would also contend that they were better mothers than certain other women because of the involvement of these inmates in this or that crime, activity, or lifestyle while they were out on the street. They cited many examples of behavior that they found "unmotherly." This included the use of drugs and child abuse. Two women stated that drug use undermined motherhood.

> *Paulette:* You know my nephew told me about his mom cooking coke in a bowl and heating it in the microwave and his brothers and sisters were watching.

> *Lonnie:* Other kids see their moms getting high and they don't get nothing, but that never happened with my kids.

Like other inmate mothers, Nicole distanced herself from other inmates whose maltreatment of children was the cause of their imprisonment.

There are people here for beating their kids and I couldn't sit here doing time and tell somebody that I did that.

Other bases for distancing from other mothers were giving birth but not caring for children and not being connected to children.

*April:* She's got nine kids and she's twenty-four years old. That's sad. She don't have any of them home. They're all under state custody. Why keep having babies like that?

*Alice:* Some women have less of a bond with their kids. You can see that on the street. There are real differences between the women here.

In putting distance between themselves and other inmate mothers, women were seeing their own performances and roles vis-à-vis their children as preferable to those of other inmates. These distinguishing marks set limits for acceptable behavior.

*Identity defended by managing challenges.* In putting distance between other mothers and themselves, inmate mothers admitted drug use and criminal activity, but many claimed higher moral ground because they did not use drugs in front of their children or did not involve them in drug sales. This hierarchy of managing drugs and children was reiterated by nearly all the drug-using women in the sample. Some claimed mothering success because their children and other adults were unaware of their involvement in crime and/or drugs. This ability to maintain role, position, and performance as mother while being engaged in criminal and drug activity meant that mothers' claims to good mothering went unchallenged despite behaviors that could have called these claims into question. April, a woman who managed a long career in prostitution, claimed that her criminal activity was effectively hidden from her partner and children.

My boyfriend who lived with me six years, he didn't know what I was going out to do [turning tricks]. So he would watch the kids. When they were older, they were in school, so I didn't have to worry about them. I would go out when they left and I came back before they came home. This way, they'd never know.

Holly and Cynthia employed stories about their children's defenses of their mothering as a way to assert their identity as good mothers despite use of drugs.

> *Holly:* My family had no idea I did drugs. My oldest son had no idea. When they came to get me, he said to the cops and the welfare worker, "My mom's not on drugs. Look at my bed. Look at my bedroom. Look at my clothes. Look at the food in my refrigerator. My friends' mothers are on drugs and those kids sleep on the floor. My mother takes care of us."

> *Cynthia:* My kids were getting into trouble at school and one of the teachers asked where the kid's mother was. My boy said that I was in jail. The school people then asked, "Does your mother have a drug problem?" My son said, "We don't know nothing about no drug problem. My mom has a shoplifting problem."

Successfully managing addiction, criminality, and motherhood meant that inmate mothers were balancing these activities without others calling into question their performances as mothers. A successful performance as mother, as evaluated by children, worked to assure mothers that despite use of drugs and criminal behavior, children were being taken care of. This is not to say that this was the case; but this strategy supported mothers' conception of good or adequate mothering.

*Identity defended by evaluating behavior and motives.* Women also assessed the behavior of other mothers in prison. Women had ample opportunities to view the mothering behavior of other inmates while incarcerated. Visits held in communal rooms, phone conversations in public places and extended visiting programs and parenting programs provided myriad chances to see and hear how other women interacted with their children. As Stacy noted, not all mothers placed children at the center of their lives.

> They talk about their kids, but they don't know what they're talking about. They make up stories about their kids. Women in here talk about their own lives, but not about their kids. I know how everything I do goes back to my kids.

Talking about children was a central feature of parenting programs at the institution. Participation in the extended visiting program required that inmates attend parenting classes and group sessions. In a group session, one woman who had served several sentences in prison had joined in a general discussion about developmental challenges facing children at specific ages. Her toddler had just turned two years old, and she expressed relief that someone else would be dealing with that stage of her child's development. The other women in the group reacted quickly, telling Barbara, "You can't say that. That's not right for you to say." There was very little tolerance for women who expressed anything but an eagerness to return to care for children, at least in some capacity. This reflected normative rules in the institution and acted to police behavior. In treatment and demonstrating fitness parlance, this was "talking the talk." Treatment staff, correctional staff, and inmates used the term "talking the talk" to refer to individuals who expressed desired sentiments and intentions but whose behaviors and actions did not match those words. In Goffman's (1959) terms, a discrepancy arises when one creates impressions that do not match the impression of self that one is attempting to give. To appear sincerely intent on changing negatively evaluated behavior, an inmate mother had to not only "talk the talk," but to "walk the walk"—that is, enroll in drug treatment and parenting programs, comply with case plans, take advantage of opportunities to see children, and other actions. This distinction between talk and action will be discussed below as we examine strategies for demonstrating fitness.

*Identity defended by bracketing.* Contrastive rhetoric was also used to separate and isolate the damaged part of mother identity from who the mother claimed to be at heart. Previous involvement in crime and drugs was bracketed and characterized as atypical behavior in the larger context of the woman's life. Marcia, a white woman with a long employment record, placed brackets around her life in prison, suggesting that this period was an aberration with little real influence on her true character.

> If I could take that two-year chunk out of my life, there wouldn't be anything different from where I am now to before all that.

Paulette made a similar observation, putting distance between her life before incarceration and her present state.

> That was the old me. I don't even like to think about it. I like the
> new me.

This strategy distinguished between problem periods in the
woman's life and isolated the threat of stigma in the past. Focusing on
recent history, Marcia argued that the determination of her fitness to
mother the child she was carrying should rest on her behavior during
her current pregnancy.

> Since I found out I was pregnant, there is nothing in my life for
> somebody to say I don't deserve to have my baby. Even though I
> have to go through all this, it's for something in the past.

Controlling threats to identity as a mother could also be achieved
by claiming that actions that might call a positive identity into question were, in fact, under control and well separated from who the
mother was in essence. Inmate mothers separated identities as mothers from identities as addicts or criminals and suggested that motherhood and mothering went on despite addiction and problems with
drugs. Some inmate mothers rejected the idea that they could not
occupy positions as good mothers and as addicts or criminals at the
same time. Yvonne also distinguished her good performance as a
mother for two of her children despite acknowledging her problems
using drugs while pregnant.

> I was using [drugs] when I was pregnant, so they charged me with
> neglect. But with the other two kids, they can't prove it's neglect, be-
> cause they were going to school, they were fed, and their appoint-
> ments were up to date. The only thing that's a problem is that I'm a user.

This suggests that mothers can be good mothers to specific children
and that assessment of good mothering is not dependent on being a
good mother to all of one's children all of the time. Lonnie, who had a
child in foster care, made a distinction between herself as a mother
and the drugs she used, suggesting that child welfare was able to make
that distinction as well.

> Child welfare has no problem with me as a mother. They have prob-
> lems with the drugs I take. If there's no drugs, there is no problem.

Women also resisted labels that were connected with criminality and rejected the idea that these labels were determinative or revealing about who they were as mothers. April made the argument that one can be on the streets (i.e., be using drugs and be involved in prostitution) and take care of children.

> Street life is hard. Real hard, but I'm used to the streets. I've done the streets almost eight years. But I can't really say that, because I took care of my kids that whole time.

Belinda, also with a long career on the streets, stated that child-welfare workers were not able to understand that one could be involved in prostitution and be a good mother simultaneously.

> They see me because I have a prostitution charge and they look at you like a prostitute and that is all that matters to them. They just don't see the mother part.

In both these instances, women placed distance between activity that identified them as sex workers and their assessment of themselves as mothers. In the case of a woman who was attempting to reclaim a child from the custody of the child-welfare agency, identification as a prostitute presented her with significant obstacles to asserting claims to motherhood. External parties, typically child-welfare workers, appeared unlikely to be able to support claims by inmate mothers to motherhood when they were known to the agency as prostitutes. Auxiliary traits associated with the master status of prostitute effectively undermined claims to motherhood. This balancing of mother and addict and criminal identities will be taken up again in a later discussion.

Talk about identity isolated or bracketed challenges to inmate mothers' claims to mother identities. In addition to identity talk, women also had to demonstrate fitness by engaging in a number of institutional programs and by taking advantage of opportunities to display mothering in this setting. These served as the basis upon which others assessed their claims to motherhood.

STRATEGIES AND ACTIONS TO PROVE FITNESS

Women in prison needed to take up a variety of actions that would allow others to assess whether their claims to motherhood were legitimate ones. It is important to note that all these strategies were indicators of demonstrating fitness and were assumed to be markers of a deeper identity—to indicate who the inmate mother really was at heart. These actions to prove fitness as mothers were constrained by the institution and by outside agents.

*Arranging visitation.* Arranging visitation provided opportunity for contact with children and also demonstrated a mother's interest in maintaining relationships with her children. For example, if the child-welfare agency was involved in the case and a determination of custody was on the horizon, inmate mothers were obliged to fulfill a variety of requirements to prove fitness. In demonstrating fitness to child-welfare staff, women had to show they were interested in their children and, in some cases, had to aggressively push the worker to arrange visits. Their need to visit with children as a means of demonstrating fitness could be frustrated by social workers who had to fit the visit into institutional schedules. Institutional rules about the length and conditions of visits also worked against "good visits" for the mothers and children. Visiting rooms were noisy and lacked privacy, and visiting times were brief. However, as artificial as these exchanges were, these visits were often the only opportunity for mother performance to be evaluated by case workers and others, other than by referring to case records.

Dilemmas arose when a young child visited a mother who may have been unfamiliar to him. He typically would become upset and cry throughout the visit. The behavior of the child would be interpreted by the worker and the mother in a variety of ways. If the child remained troubled and returned to the foster home traumatized by the encounter, the worker might be discouraged by the foster home from arranging future visits with the inmate mother. Similarly, the mother might feel overwhelmed by the visit and be tempted not to put the child through the trauma again. But to indicate an unwillingness to visit with the child might lead to a negative evaluation by the social worker. So while visiting was required to demonstrate fitness, it could easily lead to a determination that visiting (and the mother's involvement with the child) was not in the child's best interest.*

---

*Visiting by children to correctional facilities is somewhat controversial. Some believe that seeing parents in prison reduces the stigma of the environment for children

*Interest in improving parenting.* Even if child welfare was not involved, other audiences had to be satisfied. These included caretakers, children, prison staff, treatment staff, and other inmates. One of the strategies to prove fitness was to enroll in a variety of parenting classes and to participate in the extended visiting programs that were offered. Parenting programs are offered by many women's prisons in the United States and provide enhanced mother-child contact and support (Boudoris 1996). It is assumed that enhancing the connections between mothers and children will have an ameliorative impact on the criminal lifestyle of women. Many women in this study had participated in the parenting program and reported their overall satisfaction with opportunities for extended visiting with children in somewhat relaxed circumstances. Successful graduation from the parenting program indicated to program staff, child-welfare workers, and others that inmate mothers were interested in and committed to contact with children.

*Demonstrating knowledge of and interest in children.* Frequent contact with children was an indicator of fitness and provided women with information about children, not only about what they were doing in school, at home, and in other settings, but how they were doing in response to being separated from their mothers. Most women in this sample had been visited regularly by their children.** Nearly every opportunity for visiting had been taken advantage of by inmate mothers whose children's caretakers were supportive. While such frequent contact often kept the inmate mother current with the child's activities,

---

and encourages them think of prison as a "normal" environment. On the other hand, prohibiting visitation creates a significant lapse in child-parent communication that would be hard to accommodate for some children. A recent article in the *New York Times* provides a balanced account of the pros and cons of visitation programs from the perspective of prison administrators, inmate advocates, and researchers (Butterfield 1999).

**This prison may be something of an anomaly. Research by Bloom and Steinhart (1993) indicated over half of the incarcerated mothers had never been visited by their children during their incarcerations. In their research, distances between correctional facilities and the child's residence appeared to be the major factor in discouraging visitations with 60% of the population living over 100 miles from their families. In this prison, located next to bus lines in a small state, access to the prison is not hampered by geographical distance or strict administrative rules regarding visitation.

the knowledge of some mothers of details such as the age of the child, the school attended, and his or her grade level was limited and or inaccurate. In these instances, mothers overestimated how well their children were doing and underestimated the extent of problems they were encountering in school (Stanton 1980).

Some inmate mothers were aware of the dangers faced by their children in their absences. Susan knew the names of schoolteachers, who the children's friends were, and the sorts of things with which her children were struggling. Her involvement in the lives of her children had not diminished significantly because of her incarceration. Unlike other inmate mothers serving lengthy sentences, she had not successfully assigned the care of her children to others. Her steady involvement in their lives and her maintenance in the position as the children's primary caretaker was precipitated by her assessment that her husband was incompetent and unable to take care of their children. Susan had two teenage children and was in daily contact with her fifteen-year-old daughter, who had gotten pregnant and subsequently suffered a miscarriage due to an assault.

> I blame him [the girl's father] because if he would have been there and knew where she was at and who she was going with, it wouldn't have happened. I can't blame it on her. She wanted someone who would care about her so she got going with this guy.

This inmate mother was acutely aware of the challenges her three children faced in their father's care. Visits and phone calls with her children helped this woman anticipate and deal with these problems. Fitness was displayed here because she could anticipate these challenges and attempt to protect her children at a distance.

Other women were concerned about their teenage daughters. Many of the women had been sexually molested in foster homes and by family members. Their inability to be with their children to monitor potentially dangerous situations made them uneasy. This fear of children's sexual involvement was especially acute when family members seemed to be not as vigilant or sensitive to cues as were the inmate mothers. Rosa anticipated potential problems between her boyfriend and her young daughter and provided her daughter with information to afford protection that may not have been available from Rosa's mother.

I've talked with my daughter about this. I have a boyfriend who comes over and checks on my kids. He plays with them and he's really good with them. He said to my daughter that she should come over and sit on his lap and she (an eleven-year-old) told him she was too old for that. My mom felt bad for him and said his feelings were hurt, but I was proud of her.

Other mothers were concerned about the threat of gangs and the temptations of drugs for their teenage children. This was especially the case for mothers who became involved with drugs when they were young teenagers. Irene anticipated her son's encounters with drugs in junior high school and developed a plan, perhaps not a sound one, to afford protection from drug use.

My mother takes extra precautions with him because she doesn't want me coming down on her. I really worry. I'm hoping to get out of here on parole. Three more years and this child will be fourteen years old. I want to be able to correct anything that is wrong with him before it's too late. And I'm the type of person, I know I came up on drugs and alcohol and sex when I was twelve. Junior high is where it all started. So I'm thinking, I'll bring him to school. I'm small. I'll go around and see what's happening and check the gangs and the drug scene out.

The anticipation of problems demonstrated fitness for inmate mothers in that they were able to suggest potential problem areas for children and plan to address these. This is not to imply that these plans would work, but it shows that mothers understood the developmental challenges confronted by children in their absence.

The "focal concerns" of mothers precipitated by their absence reflected the age of the child and his or her relationship with caretakers. Although women with older children were concerned about dangers their children faced, mothers of infants were particularly concerned about missing key steps in the development of their young children.

*Marcia:* She's so young. She'll be just two years old when I get out. So, there's a lot of things I'm missing out on but not compared to what the rest of her life could be like.

*State of children as an indicator of maternal fitness.* In addition to enrolling in parenting programs, arranging visitation, and displaying knowledge of children, inmate mothers also demonstrated fitness by assessing the well-being of children as a result of their absence. Children were reported to be suffering emotionally due to the mother's absence. This reflected, of course, that the mother was an important figure to the child. If children remained devoted to her and missed their mother, this demonstrated that the children were attached to her, which in itself reinforced a claim to motherhood. Luisa reported her children's conversations about her and how they were dealing with emotional upset caused by her absence.

> And the kids suffer, too. They don't show it, but I know they do suffer. They miss their mom, they sure do. My mom says my daughter is always talking about me. My oldest when she sees my—sister is always getting my kids into activities—she cries. My oldest cries because she doesn't see me enough.

Yvonne's comments reflect those of mothers of teenagers and preteens who were rebelling, acting out, and angry at the absence of their mothers.

> He has a lot of anger because I'm not at home. He's had trouble in school and with his dad.

In a later section, inmate mothers' concerns about children's involvement in drugs, petty crime, truancy, teen pregnancy, and other behaviors will be discussed. Research has shown that these concerns of inmate mothers are not inappropriate, since children of parents who have been imprisoned are more likely than other children to come into contact with the criminal justice system, to drop out of school, and to become pregnant at an early age.*

Inez, a chronic recidivist, understood the impact of her long series of sentences to prison on her children.

> I can't get rid of them. I stay out for like seven months and we get close again and then I'm gone again. It always happens and it messes

---

*For an excellent review of literature on the impact of incarceration on children, and the connections between mother's imprisonment and other problem behaviors, see Johnston (1995c).

them right up again. They say, "Everybody's mother is out here but you, Ma," and it's true. I been here so many times, I'm tired of it. My kids don't want me to leave. I love my kids, though.

On other hand, some women reported their children were being well taken care of and were thriving. When inmate mothers were convinced that children were doing well, some of the mother's vigilance could be relaxed. Inmate mothers reported that because they did not worry about their children, they were able to "do the time." While this compromised the stance that mothers were unique and not replaceable, it supported the claim that children had not been seriously harmed by the mother's incarceration. Further, inmate mothers could take credit for doing "good mothering" by arranging good care for children.

*Planning for reunification.* One of the most important strategies to demonstrate fitness was planning to live with children after release from prison. This consumed considerable time and energy, especially as inmates neared their release dates. Inmate mothers planning for reunification with their children faced situations that were similar to those confronted by the homeless in joining the mainstream (Snow and Anderson 1993). In order to leave the streets, homeless individuals must find jobs; but that is contingent upon finding a place to live, which is dependent on having income, which is dependent on employment. They have limited resources with which to plan, and often their plans are somewhat vague and unrealistic. These factors contribute to their having minimal room to negotiate survival (Snow and Anderson 1993). For inmate mothers who have little social capital and few social contacts with resources, plans to reunify with children often underestimated the difficulties and challenges ahead (Baunach 1985).

Much of the planning inmate mothers did for release was constrained by institutional rules set down both by the correctional facility and by outside agencies. Some plans were contingent upon successfully completing other plans. For women involved with the child-welfare agency, successful reunification meant following a case plan. Some women could not gain return of their children until they had completed post-release residential drug treatment. Few of these programs allow mothers to live with their children, which delayed reunification and might have led to further deterioration of the mother-child relationship. In addition, child-welfare policy often imposed deadlines for inmate mothers to accomplish case plans. With the exception of women who had no prior criminal or drug involvement and who had supportive relationships with caretakers, all inmate mothers faced some contested negotiations about the return of their children with child welfare or other caretakers.

For women who had been involved in drug abuse and crime for lengthy periods of time, reclaiming children was a daunting prospect. Inmate mothers faced an array of challenges in establishing homes for children, in completing programs, and in maintaining children with caregivers while arranging independent residences. Irene, whose son had been taken care of by his grandparents since birth, was planning to assume responsibility for him upon release. She spoke about her concerns in taking on these responsibilities.

> Can I do that? Can I handle that responsibility? Can I get him to school? Get him to his appointments? Get his medicine? I need a car. I need a job. All that stuff is taken care of right now.

April's parents were also providing care for her children. Her parents had established ground rules she had to follow before she would be allowed to regain control of her children.

> They're still my kids. They're just residing with my parents until I get out. I got to stay clean for a year when I get out before I get them back. I have to stay with my mother and then get a place of my own.

Successfully planning for reunification displayed commitment to children and depended upon an inmate mother's successfully finding her way through a variety of conditions, contingencies, and requirements set down by child welfare, caretakers, and social service agencies.

*Losing children despite fitness strategies.* Despite demonstrating fitness as best as they could, some inmate women lost permanent custody of their children. That was especially likely if the children were in the care of child welfare, if other parties were interested in claiming children as their own, or if inmate mothers had extensive histories of criminal activities and drug abuse. Belinda, a prostitute and drug user, described her efforts to comply with the requirements set down by the child welfare worker to regain her son from custody.

> I worked so so hard to get my son. I took urines [urine tests] for three years. I went from a one-bedroom to a two-bedroom place. I bought the clothes. I bought the shoes. I did everything. I went to the mental health clinic so they could see how I interacted with my son, everything. I tried to do right for the worker.

Involved as a child with child welfare herself, Bernice expressed frustration with communicating with child welfare about her children, who were in foster care.

> The workers don't really try to help you. They don't tell you nothing and all of a sudden you are in court and you don't know what is happening.

Losing children to the child-welfare system or other parties meant that mothers had to adopt a new position with respect to their lost children.

### SUMMARY

Inmate mothers demonstrated fitness as a strategy to claim the identity of good mother and to make claims of ownership and rights to their children. Demonstrating fitness required identity work, and it demanded a variety of performances. Inmate mothers distanced themselves from other inmates generally (general strategies) and from particular types of inmates (specific strategies). They bracketed, defended, and isolated past behavior and identities, and replaced these with current claimed identities. Finally, inmate mothers contended that they could be both good mothers and addicts or criminals. While others, like social workers, might have been eager to equate sex work with bad motherhood, inmate mothers argued that a woman could be a prostitute and a mother and assume both identities simultaneously. How inmate mothers balance motherhood with involvement in drugs and crime will be addressed in chapter 5.

In addition to identity talk, inmate mothers engaged in activities aimed at convincing others that they were good mothers. These included arranging visits with children, enrolling in parenting programs, displaying knowledge of children, and planning for reunification. Typically, these strategies did work to establish that the inmate was a good mother, or to make her mothering not subject to further investigation. However, in some cases, despite an inmate mother's completion of all program requirements and her efforts to reestablish identity as good mother, she would lose custody of her child to the state or to other caretakers. Work to demonstrate fitness was indicative of the fact that children were a contested resource and subject to negotiations among the mother, caretakers, child welfare, and others.

## NEGOTIATING OWNERSHIP OF CHILDREN

Children serve as resources in a number of ways. Children are resources in that they are "priceless" innocents (Zelizer 1985) and carry social value (Day and Mackey 1988). As discussed in the previous section, children worked to substantiate mother identity, which could serve as a major counterweight to identity as a "typical inmate." For inmate mothers who had little social or economic capital, children were viewed as the only remaining resource they had. In terms of changing addictive or criminal careers, children could be used by mothers and others as incentives to modify and alter behavior. Finally, children served as resources for women to repair damaged identities as mothers.

Of course, children were burdens, as well. They presented demands for care. They required attention and financial support. They reflected to some degree the status of their parents and the relationships within the family they were born into. Finally, children were burdens with respect to identity. Mothers had to account for children and their care. A lack of accounting—that is, of not being responsible—put women's claims to mother identity, role, and position into jeopardy. Given their value and their cost, children were the subject of battles over who "owned" them and who should be in control.

*Children as burdens to families.* Children were seen as burdens in some families. For example, Irene, a white woman who bore a child out of wedlock as a teenager, interpreted caretaking of her son as a burden to her mother.

> She resents the fact that she has to take care of him and I don't blame her. But she only stepped in so he wouldn't go to foster care. He is a real handful and she's not that young anymore.

As noted in chapter 2, white grandparents were typically characterized as taking care of children out of sacrifice. Parents with adult children were expected to be enjoying themselves or attending to demands and interests other than child rearing. Expectations of caretaking for grandchildren were different for African American women, who maintained that children were not seen as burdens in the way this was understood in the white community. This was the case even when caring for additional children in households meant serious financial strain.

*Children as resources to communities.* Inmate mothers from communities of color were more likely to consider their children as resources. As Collins (1990) has noted, "ownership" of children is an issue that is different in black and white communities. While black families are likely to rely on informal adoption to provide short- and long-term care of children (Martin and Martin 1978), white families are less willing to extend support for residential and nonresidential child care. Further, white children are not often seen as resources to, or the responsibility of, the larger community. Responsibility for white children is more likely to be confined to the nuclear family unit.

In contrast, black women in prison often saw children as helping older female family members to maintain important roles. Inez, a chronic offender, suggested that taking care of children was just what her mother needed to do at this stage of her life.

> But she loves it. I think it keeps her living. It makes you realize she would probably die without those kids.

Other African American women noted that distant relatives and others would offer to care for children in need of homes because they felt children were valuable and and that no child should go to foster care.

*Children as the only thing women have left.* As inmate mothers assessed their status as inmates, many traced their careers as mothers and members of the community as following a downward trajectory.

The great majority of women in this study were located at economic and social margins, although, in some cases, the economic rewards of crime enhanced a family's financial status for a short time. Some who had been employed and lived comfortably with their children before imprisonment characterized themselves as "losing everything" to crime and drugs. After incarceration, the women had few resources with which to rebuild a life in the community. For women with limited resources and minimal social margin, children endured as their only remaining social capital. Nicole reported the losses she suffered because of her involvement in drugs and eventual conviction on a drug-trafficking charge.

> I had everything. I had a car, a house, a job, my kids. Now look at me. All I got left are my kids and we'll have to start all over again.

Susan and Inez also saw children as the only resource that is left to women whose lives have been destroyed by drugs and crime.

> *Susan:* A lot of times, the kids are all a woman has. If they would just look at the bond before they would take kids. That's all these women have.

> *Inez:* I would kill someone for my kids. That's my world. I can't function without them.

Having children—that is, not having them taken away by the state—established a base line for inmate mothers to measure how far they had fallen from previous identities and social standing. Children as the only remaining social good also served as a resource around which mothers could start reestablishing positions and roles as mothers.

*Children as resources for change.* Besides the value of children as resources in relation to mother's identity, children were also seen as valuable obstacles to drug use and crime and as reasons for changing behavior. Several women, including Belinda, linked loss of children to child welfare or other caretakers as trigger events for addiction and criminality.

> I really honestly believe that because they took my kids away, it just strained me out. To take my child away is to give me every reason to use.

Tee and Alice identified children as the reason for changing behaviors.

> *Tee:* I'm not going to jail no more. I'm not gonna to do this no more because if I do, I'm gonna lose my kids for good.
>
> *Alice:* What keeps me strong is my kids. It was when I stopped using that I became a good mother.

The prospect of mothering in the future had redemptive value for inmate mothers who had failed in mothering in the past. Doing good mothering for one child had enormous import for the mother's assessment of her mothering ability. Assessments of future success with children were not linked to previous mother work, which in some cases had been appropriated by others and, in some cases, had been a failure. Nicole admitted her lack of connection to her first child although she remained in contact with her.

> My daughter I didn't raise. I didn't really want that baby. I love her more than anything and I wouldn't trade her for nothing and she's absolutely beautiful. She sticks her tongue out at me and she doesn't like me because I gave her away.

Like Nicole, Beth expressed her lack of attachment to her oldest child.

> When she was born, I knew I was supposed to love her. I didn't have any feelings like a mother should. My mother has those feelings for her.

For many women who were pregnant, the prospect of having a baby was restorative, a second chance at "motherhood." Paulette and Beth, for instance, placed great hopes in the upcoming birth of their children.

> *Paulette:* When I see him I see all of them and the future we are having together. I see all of them in him. I couldn't be there for the rest of them, but at least I can try with him.
>
> *Beth:* When I think about this baby, I see him bringing us all together. I am getting clean for this baby.

While mothers saw a new baby as a new chance to mother, they also indicated that older children resented their late start at good parenting.

One teenage girl asked her mother why she didn't give up drugs and prostituting earlier. While mothers may see multiple chances to do good mothering, the perspective of children may be quite different, especially as they weigh the commitment of mothers to themselves as children and compare it to that shown to other siblings.

OWNERSHIP OF CHILDREN

Not all women faced battles over the care and custody of their children. A significant number of women maintained central places in the lives of children before, during, and after incarceration. For these women, incarceration meant only a temporary displacement in relationships with children. With supportive caretakers of their children, women were assured that their relationships and positions with respect to their children would not be weakened significantly while they were in prison. For some other women, however, incarceration opened up significant threats from others over ownership of children. Caretakers attempted to replace mothers in their roles and positions and worked to legally terminate their rights to the children. Ownership of children became a bargaining issue incumbent upon the mother's conforming to requirements set down by others.

Even when inmate mothers maintained custody of children and were involved in their lives, they expressed concern over their lack of primary relationships with children. Ownership of children was an issue in families where the primary relationship to children was typically thought to be confined to only one adult (usually the mother). Typically, these lines of ownership were most explicit in white families. For women of color, ownership of children was usually less of an issue, but did become an issue when caretakers drew lines that limited the involvement of the mother in the lives of her children.

*Battles over children.* Battles over children typically arose when children were taken care of by others because the mother was unable to provide care (appropriation) or when mothers were unable to exert power over hostile caregivers (incarceration effects). Children might have been appropriated while the mother was unable to care for children due to illness, addiction, or involvement with crime and the criminal justice system. Beth, Vanessa, and Irene all spoke of how their newborns were appropriated by their mothers at birth because of their own inability to care for these children.

> *Beth:* She just took the baby from the hospital. I was serving a sentence then. She tried to fool me and I never forgot that feeling of having that baby taken away.

> *Vanessa:* He has always been her baby. I never had a chance. Ever since he was born, he was her baby.

> *Irene:* I was seventeen when my son was born and he stayed with me for a while till I was just so out of control that my mother took over. He's been there ever since.

For some women, this appropriation was seen in retrospect as perhaps the best arrangement under the circumstances but unfair because the mother had no say in the decision. Some appropriations left the mother with no way to regain a central place in the child's life unless the caretaker decided to let her or unless the caretaker was unable to continue providing for the child.

Women serving long sentences also faced threats to their status as mothers from caretakers who were not supportive. One Hispanic woman, Rachel, was fighting to maintain custody of her children, who were living with her husband outside of the United States. She described the battle as follows:

> My husband took my kids back to the islands when I came here. They had grown up in this country. While I am here, he tried to get custody of my kids. I think his sister is behind it, because she don't have kids of her own. She acts like she's their mother and my husband don't care. That just makes less work for him.

This battle over children resulted in the mother's losing more ground with the children and, given her lengthy sentence, there were few measures that she could mount to effectively win this contest over the children.

*Lines of ownership.* Lines of ownership of children were drawn quite clearly in some families. Determining who owned children was not just an issue when relationships between inmate mothers and caretakers were hostile. In some instances, inmate mothers felt that because other care-takers asserted primary caretaking roles, usually reserved for mothers, they needed to mark ownership of subsequent children. For white mothers, like Marcia, this often suggested that once others established a primary relationship with children early in their lives, mothers could not regain lost ground with children as their primary caretakers.

> I was telling my husband. This one is his. The next one will be all mine.

Children here are clearly the "property" of one parent or the other, not both.

*Losing battles and maintaining connections.* Even though women had lost battles over children, they sometimes maintained claims to mother-hood through biological connections. Black women in this study at-tributed little meaning or weight to the legal termination of rights to children. Although the child-welfare system and the courts had offi-cially severed relationships between the mothers and their children, the women argued that they could maintain connected to their chil-dren in other ways. They maintained that their bonds with their chil-dren were so strong that the law and its workings would have little impression on the children. When the children were old enough, they would seek out their mothers and determine the direction of relation-ships with them. This belief was maintained even when children were adopted by individuals unknown to the mother and there had been minimal contact for several years. Although most women saw termi-nation of parental rights as a significant threat to their mothering chil-dren, Susan did not expect this legal action would have any effect on her relationship with her teenage children.

> They [child welfare] could do that legally [terminate her rights] but my kids aren't going to pay any attention to that.

Margaret, Paulette, and Belinda, all of whom had had legal rights ter-minated by the state, asserted they would eventually be reconciled with their children.

*Margaret:* I know they will come looking for me and that I am doing everything I can to get them back.

*Paulette:* I look forward to seeing them someday and telling them all about my story.

*Belinda:* Like how can you terminate the rights of a mother to a kid when she had that kid [gave it birth]? What's going to happen is that when Jackie is old enough to come to me, she'll come to me. My mother says children always do. She will come to me because my aunt always denied me going there.

So, although other caretakers had gained legal rights to children, the loss of children to others was thought temporary because of the special and unbreakable connections between mothers and their children.

### SUMMARY

Children provided inmate mothers with opportunities to assert positive identities and to claim statuses as "normal" women. However, the fact of children also suggested that inmate mothers were not "normal" women in that their criminality and addiction called into question their commitment and attachment to their children and to their mother role. Battles over children were engaged when caretakers and others became concerned about the mother's ability to provide care for the children for whom she was responsible. Mothers often provoked these concerns when they became involved with drugs, alcohol, and criminality. Although one claimed identity as a mother, serious involvement in drugs and crime tended to undermine that claim and pushed women to take some actions to preserve at least a semblance of a right to claim a positive identity as a mother. The construction of motherhood and mothering while incarcerated presents an important facet of how mothering is done. How motherhood, addiction, and criminality are balanced is the focus of chapter 5.

# Chapter 5

# Constructing and Managing Motherhood, Drugs, and Crime

Although dominant ideology proposes that mothers must be the sole caretakers of their children and that failure to properly conduct mother work will result in damaged children, women increasingly have been pushed to assign others the care of their children. This shared child keeping has long been a feature of black communities (Collins 1990) and communities of color but has only recently characterized middle-class white families. How women manage and understand relationships with child-care providers affords important insights into how women in prison may come to understand and interpret their relationships with others who were taking care of their children. As we will see below, women maintained identities as "good mothers" even while others were providing the bulk of daily care for children. This section will also examine how inmate mothers established connections to children, identified unique positions for themselves with respect to children, and constructed ideas about "good mothering."

The "moral career" (Goffman 1961) of women inmates can be examined in a number of ways. The use of the term "career" provides a way to explore commitment to the position, role, and work of mother and to consider it as a part-time, sporadic, full-time, or suspended activity before and during incarceration. We can also follow the trajectory of careers as women managed identities as inmates and mothers.

For most women confined to a correctional facility, imprisonment prompted some change in the mother role vis-à-vis the child and others. As argued in chapter 2, identity as a mother was a valuable resource, especially for women inmates, since it countered or challenged the inmate-criminal-addict identity. As Goffman (1961) noted, when individuals withdraw from a situated self, they do not create new psychological worlds, but instead act in the name of some other socially created identity. Inmate mothers were challenged to maintain identity as "good mothers" in a context where barriers to claim that identity were multiple. Typically, commitment to a role requires regular performance of duties associated with that role. Absence of the mother from daily care of her children undermines the validity of her claim to good motherhood. Inmate mothers' claims to good motherhood were challenged by this and also by their involvement in crime, especially if that involvement was serious and chronic. The very fact of imprisonment threatened claims to good motherhood, because the women had committed offenses that led to their separation from children in the first place.

## CONSTRUCTING AND MANAGING MOTHERHOOD

For a small number of women, imprisonment meant little disruption in the lives of their children. Arrangements with caretakers had been established to provide care for children on an ongoing basis and there was permanent substitute care. These women either arranged caretaking by family or husbands, or made placements through child welfare. These women sometimes adopted a relationship to their children in which contact was erratic equivalent to a non-custodial father where contact was erratic and, in some instances, behavior was indulgent. If caretakers became dissatisfied or exhausted with the burden of care, they could pressure the mother to resume child care. If that was unsuccessful, family members and others could push the case to resolution by engaging the services of child welfare. In some instances, this worked as a lever to force the mother to change her behavior. In extreme cases, the rights of the mother to the child were legally terminated, resulting in the formal adoption of the child. When children were adopted by persons who were unknown to the mother, inmate mothers referred to this as "losing children to the state."

Commitment to a role requires regular performance of that role and its associated duties (Goffman 1961). As women's ties to children weakened by virtue of their lack of involvement in day-to-day management of children, their identities as mother weakened as well, thus freeing them up for continued involvement in criminal and drug activity (McGowan and Blumenthal 1978). Caretakers eliminated some mothers from decision making for children, leading to the mother's becoming somewhat peripheral to the family unit. Martin (1997) reported the virtual disappearance of women from families when they became noncustodial mothers of children. In a five-year follow-up study, 33 percent of women who were released from prison had lost custody of their children. These women, referred to as "non-custodial mothers" by Martin, persisted in lifestyles that included chronic drug use and crime. These mothers were unable to follow case plans set down by child welfare and were found to be neglecting and abusing children. While the loss of custody may have been a good marker for categorizing relationships between women and their children, it was also apparent in this study that women and caretakers resorted to a variety of arrangements that did not include formal legal procedures or agency involvement. Custody or the lack of it masked a variety of arrangements. In some instances, grandmothers adopted the children, yet the mother remained in daily contact and would resume living with the child upon release. In other instances, mothers retained full custody while never having taken major responsibility for children.

*Mothering and pregnancy.* Women make a number of claims to motherhood. For many women, pregnancy marks the beginning of the development of identification with motherhood (Rothman 1987; McMahon 1995). Many women see pregnancy as a period in which they assume obligations for care of their developing children. This view is shared by various agencies of social control and the law.*

Using illicit drugs during pregnancy has been found to violate a "fundamental feeling rule" among drug-using women (Kearney and

---

*There are an increasing number of laws that criminalize activities by mothers that are considered to place fetuses in danger. These include drug and alcohol use during pregnancy. There has been significant debate about these laws and whether they seek to protect children or are an effort to criminalize behavior that is more suitable for medical intervention (Maher 1992). Golden (1997) notes that, given the limited availability of drug treatment for pregnant women, criminalizing drug abuse and treating it as child abuse as well makes addressing this issue more problematic for mothers, their children, and caseworkers.

Murphy 1993). Many women in this study noted pregnancy as a special period during which they took extra care to remain drug-free. This was especially the case if other children had been removed from the woman's care by the state or by relatives and if the woman wished to raise the child. Beth, a woman who was three months pregnant, provoked an arrest that she knew would lead to incarceration.

> I was drinking and just relapsed. I was a prostitute, getting high and doing cocaine. My boyfriend was hitting me, too. So, I flagged down a car and got busted by the cops. I am happy to be here and knew that if I came here the baby would be OK.

For this woman, imprisonment during the pregnancy demonstrated good mothering, because she had avoided temptation and pressures of the street that could have undermined a healthy pregnancy. In addition, because she had served an earlier sentence, the prospect of imprisonment did not appear frightening or daunting to her. It represented role distance from her work as a prostitute and an embracing of the mother identity in prison.

*Motherhood established by giving birth.* Women also claimed motherhood by virtue of having given birth, of course, but that was not always accompanied by their taking care of children or by having legal custody of them. Claims by others to motherhood based on professional knowledge, on legal determination of motherhood by the courts, or on current or past caretaking of one's children were dismissed in favor of biological connections to children. Paulette, a mother of six children, reflected the sentiments of women who privileged the giving of birth to children over all other claims to motherhood.

> These people in the drug program say that I'm a bad parent because I don't know how to take care of kids. I know how to take care of kids. I been baby-sitting since I been six years old. I think if you haven't given birth to children, you really don't know nothing about children.

Two inmate mothers made clear distinctions between taking care of children and being the children's mother. Caretaking here was equated with "custodial" care, as used by Uttal (1994), referring to the mere housing and keeping of children but not the connected caring that mothers would provide.

> *Belinda:* Those are my kids. They are not my aunt's kids. She may have had them, and kept them and nourished them and loved them and stuff, but these are my kids.

> *April:* They're still my kids. They're just residing at my mother's house until I get out.

Margaret's comments were typical of women whose claims to being mothers rested on biology when rights to children had been terminated or were in the process of being terminated. All seven of Margaret's children had been adopted by others. The legal termination of her rights to them did not in any way diminish her feeling of "ownership" of them.

> Those are my kids. They may be taken away, but that don't mean nothing.

This claim of motherhood and connection remained strong even when the mothers admitted that other providers were good parents to children and that their own performance as mothers was compromised by serious drug or alcohol use. Inmate mothers resisted the labeling by agencies of social control and others that they were bad mothers.

*Mothers and children as knowing each other.* Inmate mothers also claimed that children knew them as mothers even though there had been minimal face-to-face interaction. Inmate mothers suggested that just as mothers always know their children, children also always know who their mothers are. Implied was a unique and singular bond between mothers and their children. Belief in this was illustrated in a conversation between two inmate mothers when an infant was visiting his mother in the parenting program.

> *Holly:* Does this baby know his mom?
> *Lonnie:* Of course he does. Babies have a sense. They always know their mothers. Didn't you know that?
> *Holly:* I did, but I just wanted to hear it again.

Some mothers, separated from their children at birth, struggled with their relationships to children. Inmate mothers distinguished between ways of knowing and being known by their children. Children knew mothers as individuals in their lives but not as their primary caretakers. Lonnie, whose child was in foster care, drew a clear line between her child recognizing her and his knowing her as his primary caretaker, his mother.

> My son visits me here. He knows me but he doesn't *know* me, *know* me. I mean he knows who I am, but he doesn't know me in that way.

In situations where a baby had been taken into foster care by child welfare at birth or where the mother had given birth just prior to coming to prison, women had limited sustained contact with children. As Theresa and Luisa said, there are instances in which children do not recognize their mothers as significant figures in their lives.

> *Theresa:* My daughter's probably thinking I'm just some lady she comes to visit.

> *Luisa:* I had him just six months before I came to jail, so I don't think he knows me at all.

Women typically worried that children would not recognize them as their mothers. Although they laid claim to a special and unique position in the lives of their children, they were also faced with the fact that their performance as mothers had been severely limited by their absence in the lives of their children. The result of this lack of performing as mother was especially acute in cases where very young children did not recognize their mothers as special and unique figures and instead equated "mother" with their current caretaker.

*Maintaining and undermining mother's place.* Caretakers and others either supported identification of the birth mother as the mother of the child or undermined that in some way. Children sometimes called other women "Mom" and called their mothers by their first names. Some children could accommodate multiple "mothers" and could distinguish these caretakers from each other quite readily. Managing identity and position as mother was very often the result of negotiations with caretakers. In some instances, arranging child care resulted in the inmate mother's limiting her role with respect to her children. Women had to manage their roles vis-à-vis those who were caring for their children because of prior agreements and territory staking.

In cases where an adoptive caretaker did not wish to disclose the mother's biological relationship to the child, inmate mothers had to walk a fine line between being a presence in the child's life and not acting like the child's mother. This included not exerting or vying for control, deferring to the judgment of others, and seeing the child at the discretion of the caretakers. In many instances, caretakers could exercise control over the content and extent of involvement the mother had with the children, because the mother was interested in maintaining some contact with her children and was willing to abide by conditions set by the caretaker. These conditions, as explained by three inmate mothers, restricted their relationships and contact with their children. Some of these were put in place by relative caretakers; others by the state.

> *Belinda:* I love my aunt to death, but she kept my daughter from me for five years. I don't want to go through that again with my son.

> *Nicole:* So, as far as the state and my mother is concerned, I'm not to have any contact with them if my mother chooses not to, but they come every Saturday to the parenting program here and I call them once a week.

> *Paulette:* I can't go to my mother's house to see my son because my daughter's there. Child welfare don't want me seeing her.

These situations were difficult to manage because children who were available for mothering—that is, those not freed for adoption or already adopted—were living with brothers or sisters whose status vis-à-vis the mother had already been severed, at least legally. Until these situations were worked out, the mother and the caretaker had to negotiate appropriate roles, positions, and performances. However, if the mother failed to make and maintain contact with her children, her claim to them was further undermined. In these cases, a mother was faced with the dilemma of putting the judgment of others about what was best for her children before her own wishes. If other caretakers were considered better care providers by significant audiences (child welfare, family members, the mother herself), "good" mothers had to concede their rights to make decisions about their children. But if mothers were still interested in and committed to children and the mother role with respect to them, contact and repeated attempts at that were requisites to any real hope for reunification.

*What mothers do.* As indicated in the mainstream literature on motherhood, women are confronted with a variety of messages about motherhood. Cultural messages about what mothers are supposed to do and be are multiple and often contradictory. Inmate mothers' ideas about parenting and motherhood reflected some of the mainstream ideology about what a good mother is and does (LeFlore and Holston 1990). Some of their comments about the characteristics of a good mother included "Mothers are always there," "Mothers are strong," and "Mothers are understanding." Inmate mothers characterized good mothers as central figures in the lives of their children, as confidantes, teachers, friends, the focus of love, and the person who should help children understand right from wrong. Black and Hispanic women identified fewer differences between themselves and their own mothers in ideas about child rearing and motherhood than did white women. In addition, black women were likely to identify their own mothers as role models for good mothering, which few white women did.

*Managing motherhood at a distance.* Attempting to mother at a distance presented inmate mothers with a number of challenging situations. They had to see to it that others were providing good care for their children and that certain tasks were performed. Because inmate mothers had varying ideas about what mothers do, they also had different standards about what caretakers should have been doing in their absence. If what the mothers had done consisted of minimal care, like sheltering, feeding, and clothing children, the mothers were likely to assume that similar arrangements were adequate for their children. Focusing on the tasks associated with routine care of children, Irene reported her satisfaction with the care provided to her son.

> My son is clothed and fed. He gets what he needs and then some, sometimes when they [her elderly, ill parents] can't afford it.

If inmate mothers saw little difference between what they and other caretakers did with respect to children, they were more likely to be satisfied with care. However, when inmate mothers conceived of mothering as all-engaging—that is, with the mother as the emotional center of the child's life and being—chances were that they were deeply concerned about the effect of their absence from children. It was also likely that they were dissatisfied with the care the children were receiving. Displeasure with child care was also probable, of course, when mothers saw caretakers as hostile and incompetent.

Despite inmate mothers' efforts to maintain a significant role in the lives of their children, the fact was that they were living apart from children, except for a few hours a week when visiting. This meant that the women, their children, and the caretakers had to balance distance and attachment. In some instances, the women opted to reduce contact on their part. They stepped back from "mothering" and recognized that their involvement with their children would be minimal and severely limited during incarceration. Women suggested that in order to "do the time" inmate mothers had to give up thinking that were in control of managing their children and their caretakers. Belinda noted the difficulty of being in prison and being a force in the lives of her children.

> It's hard because I'm there and I'm not there. I mean they think about me but they have a lot going on. Sometimes I think it's better not to call, because it gets everybody upset, especially me.

In some instances, as Rosa and Nicole stated, maintaining contact with children accentuated the pains of imprisonment and emphasized the fact that children's lives were continuing despite the mother's imprisonment.

> *Rosa:* Sometimes I just don't feel like calling. It's just too sad. I try to keep in touch, but sometimes it's just too much.

> *Nicole:* That's why for a long time I didn't call my house, like for three weeks, because I didn't want to hear about it, what was going on. I didn't care if they were having fun or where they were going.

Alternatively, women opted to minimize emotional pain by putting their concerns about children in abeyance. This strategy placed distance between inmate mothers and their children and suggested that because children were in the care of others, women were relatively powerless to affect their treatment. Minimizing contact and placing performance as a mother in suspense directed responsibility for children to others and put it out of the mother's hands, except for involvement as an interested party. In many instances, it became problematic for inmate mothers to demonstrate their interest in children while also understanding and recognizing the pains of separation for those children. Lee expressed this dilemma with respect to her children.

> They think that I don't hang them up [pictures of her children] because I couldn't be bothered. That hurts. For me, it hurts for me to see my kids in pictures and stuff and I'm not there. You know what I'm saying? I can't. I can't look at them. I feel so guilty. I can't look at their pictures and not feel so guilty.

Although inmate mothers missed children and wished they were closer, expression of this loss had be managed lest it overwhelm women who could do little to change the situation they were in. Because children's lives went on despite the imprisonment of their mothers, inmate mothers had little choice but to adjust their expectations of what relationships with children would be like during their incarceration.

*Mothering as unique and not replaceable.* Some inmate mothers considered their relationships with and caretaking of children unique and not replaceable. Kathy, a white inmate mother of a six-year-old, was very supportive of her husband's ability to accomplish a great deal of what needed to be done to take care of their child. Although she commended him on his cooking, cleaning, and general child care, she distinguished between how a mother does mothering and how her husband performed the same work. Her husband and her son had gone shopping for school clothes.

> I looked at what they picked out and thought to myself, "My God, I would have never bought such a thing for him." No mother would have.

Despite her husband's more than adequate execution of caretaking tasks, Kathy claimed that a mother's performance would have been different. It would, she thought, have made this task of buying shoes a different experience—in other words, mother work involves task performance and emotion work that only mothers can do.

Other inmates also suggested that mothers were central figures in the lives of their children. Tee suggested that a father is not a substitute for a mother.

> Kids need their mother. They can go with their father OK but they really need their mother.

Inez discussed the importance of telling her children that she loved them despite her imprisonment.

> We just do everything together and I just love them. I tell them that constantly over and over. Every time I call I try to drill it into their heads. They want it to be me and them.

Some women contended that mothers were not replaceable as figures in their children's lives. If they were irreplaceable, this would mean that the children were being seriously harmed by their incarceration. Mothers conceded that other providers could feed, clothe, and support children. They also admitted that many other caretakers loved their children and provided excellent care for them. However, inmate mothers claimed that mothers cared for children in a special way and that they, as mothers, had exclusive and unique relationships with respect to children.

*Mothers as different from and similar to other caretakers.* Inmate mothers also distinguished their work and ideas about good mothering from what other caretakers did. Many caretakers were middle-aged and older and were reported to have less patience than did mothers themselves. Caretakers also controlled what children watched on television and imposed curfews and other rules. Some inmate mothers contended that caretakers indulged children more or less than they did. Because Rosa and Irene, both involved in the drug trade, had had access to significant economic resources by virtue of their crimes, their children experienced a higher standard of living when their mothers were around.

*Rosa:* My kids say to me, "We don't go nowhere. If you were here, we know we would be going to Disney World or on vacation." I feel bad because I know when I get out that will be all over.

*Irene:* I got to tell my kid we can't do that no more. We just don't have it. He only wants the best sneakers. My father bought him some good ones and he cut them up because they weren't the ones he wanted. He said he would wait till I got out to go shopping. I had to talk with him about that and set him straight.

Few caretakers were able to provide what mothers did in terms of "treats," vacations, clothing, and high-priced sneakers. This caused some problems with children and their caretakers.

*Mothers and quality time.* In some instances, women who were seriously committed to a criminal and drug lifestyle had spent little time in the community living with their children. For example, Inez, an inmate mother had come to prison to serve more than ten sentences over a twenty-year period, maintained that she provided her children with very focused attention for an intense but limited period of time.

Even if you don't give them too much attention, like me. I haven't been there that much in their lives. But when I'm there, I am really with them.

The quality of these relationships with children—albeit limited in time—were seen as superior to the routine daily care afforded by other caretakers.

*Mother work done by others.* In instances in which the inmate mother was living with her children prior to imprisonment, a realignment in family roles and responsibilities in the family necessarily occurred upon her incarceration. Absence of the mothers meant that the children had to assume more responsibilities, especially in kin-based arrangements. Rosa described the responsibilities her oldest daughter assumed, which included caretaking and supervision of younger children.

She's eleven and real smart. Sometimes, she gets mad at me. She says, "Mom, why did you have so many kids, because now I'm stuck with them?" It's true, I feel sad because sometimes she wants to go outside and play, but my son is only three and can't be alone. If my mother is not home, she has to stay in the house with him. She gets mad because she's old enough to be outside playing and not watching a three-year-old. That's the only reason she gets mad. She has to help, because me and my mom can't always be watching the kids. So that's the only reason she gets mad at me. She sometimes asks, "Mom, why are you there?"

For other families, arrangements to get necessary family work done were established and routine, and persisted upon the return of the imprisoned mother to the community. This work was done not only because the children were old enough to do the work but also because their assessment of the mother was that she was not able to accomplish this parental work. Inez, a drug dealer, described how finances were managed in her house.

If I get a lot of money, I give it to my son to take hold of. Whenever I have money, they [her children] don't leave the house. They always ask me where I put it, what I'm doing with it. I'm telling you, I have some strange kids. Not strange, but they act like they own me.

In these instances, as children grew older, they began to understand and incorporate the mother's household work as their own in order to gain some control over their lives.

*Mother work left undone.* Despite the work that inmate mothers did in selecting, arranging, and managing child care, the women typically found that important work remained undone. Frequently, the women recognized that their children were not being adequately protected or supervised. Lee expressed, her concern about child molestation and felt that her children were in danger because other caretakers were not as protective as she.

'Cause I'm always thinking someone's gonna touch them or something. It's hard because they're not with me and I'm not there to protect them.

This concern over protection of children was evident with women whose children lived in neighborhoods where they were likely to run into trouble but whose caretakers were without the "street smarts" necessary to recognize danger signs. Theresa, aware of the dangers on street, feared that her mother would not be able to handle a situation involving violence against her child.

> I know my mother does her best. She would never put him in a dangerous situation, but what will she be able to do if there's a drive-by shooting and one of them gets hit? These are the things I worry about.

As Susan and Stacy noted, caretakers may be "streetwise" but still unlikely to provide a level of care or supervision the mother thought was necessary. Caretakers have problems of their own and limitations, as well, which undermine their abilities to provide the sort of care mothers would like to have available.

> *Susan:* Well, I thought maybe he could handle it and they would be treated all right and that he could keep up what I had started—like the discipline. If they needed the help, the loving, even little things, but he hasn't done any of that. For the past eight months, I would tell them over the phone that if they didn't go to school, they couldn't go out, then can't go to friends', those friends can't come over. Two hours later, I would call and he would have let them out. And when he did that, my kids wouldn't listen. They started not listening to me either and they started running the streets. I would call and he would say, "Well, I don't know where they are."
>
> *Stacy:* I call him up to check on things. Sometimes, he'll be high and he's telling me him and my son are going somewhere. I want to kill him because he is high and he's getting into a car with my son. There's nothing I can do about it.

From the distance of prison, the mothers were relatively powerless to exert control over the individuals who shared custody of the children.

SUMMARY

In constructing and managing roles and identities as inmate mothers, women put forth claims to motherhood. There were several bases for these claims. Biological connections to motherhood by vir-

tue of giving birth were always available as a resource to claim identity. Claims to motherhood also rested on the staking out of special or
unique relationships to children that could not be appropriated by
caretaking others. Concerns about children in the hands of bad caretakers reaffirmed mothers' claims to motherhood by suggesting that
their absence led to the child's suffering harm. Typically, the work
that mothers did in attempting to "mother" apart from children meant
that they had to effectively manage caretakers and others. For some
women, reclaiming children totally (the inmate mother taking major
responsibility for child care) or in part (the inmate mother sharing
care of the child) from caretakers rested on the inmate mother's ability to balance crime, drugs, and motherhood.

## BALANCING CRIME, DRUGS, AND MOTHERHOOD

In this analysis, we have employed Goffman's (1961) term "moral career" to understand how women inmates maintained identities as
mothers. It is useful to think of crime and drug use as "work" to be
accomplished. In combining careers as mothers and criminals and/or
addicts, women faced significant obstacles. Maintaining self-identity
as a "good mother" is a challenge for conventional mothers who juggle
child care and work responsibilities. For inmate mothers, balancing
"work" and family was even more difficult. In this section, I will discuss the impact of incarceration on the families of inmate mothers, on
the separation of inmate/addict/criminal careers from motherhood, and
the effect of balancing addiction, crime, and motherhood on mother
careers.

*Inmate mothers under supervision.* Correctional sanctions required
families to adjust to incarceration. These necessarily had an impact
on children and other family members. As families responded to crises, there was often a shifting of roles and work that had to be done
within the family unit. These changes meant that generational and
gender roles had to be rearranged to accommodate changes in the
family. Children occupied adult roles, deviant adults were treated as
children, and husbands or partners did work traditionally performed

by wives. Incarceration itself placed the mother in the position of having her behavior monitored and supervised by correctional staff as
well as by her family and children. Children who were visiting mothers in correctional facilities learned about the various rules to which
mothers were subject. They learned that if mothers did not comply
with certain rules, they would be unable to visit and the mothers would
be unable to make a phone call home. Several researchers (Johnston
1995c) have found that incarceration undermines parental authority.
Rosa explained how her position as mother was undermined by her
children's questioning her about her behavior.

> I usually call the house everyday. When they don't visit, I call. But if
> I don't call, they think I am in trouble. So, when I call the next day,
> they say, "Mom, you been in trouble? You didn't call." So, I say,
> "No, I been good." And my daughter says, "Oh, sure, Mom," and I
> say, "I been good." I never been in trouble. Sometimes, I just don't
> feel like calling, they always ask me about being good.

Most children were aware that their mothers were in a correctional setting, and many young children attributed this to their mother's
making a mistake, breaking the law, or being "sick." Such a public
recognition that the mother had been "bad" put children in the position of telling the mother how to behave and to how avoid further
incarceration. This especially seemed to be the case for older children, who perceived more accurately than their younger siblings did
the real reason for their mother's incarceration.

Conversations with children in the visiting program provide insight
here. Previous research has demonstrated that as children of inmates
grow older they may be increasingly resentful and angry at parental
absence (Kampfner 1995; McGowan and Blumenthal 1978). An inmate who had been in and out of prison throughout the childhood of
her six children was about to be released. Her oldest child, a seventeen-year-old girl, had been managing the household and supervising
her three younger brothers and sisters. Sherill had developed a strategy to limit her mother's disruption of her home.

> *Enos:* Who takes care of the kids?
> *Sherill:* I do.
> *Enos:* Who takes care of the baby?

*Sherill:* I do.

*Enos:* Who takes care of your mother?

*Sherill:* She does, just her. I feel bad about her being in prison, but there's nothing I can do, is there? This goes on all the time. This time we decided if she shows up at our house high and strung out, we just won't let her in.

As previously mentioned, for some families the return of the offender signaled disruption in lives they had constructed in the offender's absence. Other family members had taken over responsibilities in the household, had imposed order and had managed family resources, perhaps more predictably and equitably than had the mother.

As women reflected on previous careers as mothers, offenders, and addicts, they compared themselves to other inmate mothers, positioning themselves on a hierarchy of addict-criminal-mother identity. Typically, inmate mothers compared themselves to other mothers and suggested that others were less worthy than they were of the title of "good mother." Mothers who had only committed property crimes ranked higher in the worthiness hierarchy than those who were prostitutes. Mothers who used drugs but who did not involve children were placed at the next level down. Women who employed children as helpers in drug sales and those who used drugs in front of children were at the next level, near the bottom of the hierarchy. Women who made no accommodation for their children when they knew they had serious problems with drugs were placed at the bottom of the hierarchy. The criteria for ranking mothers in this hierarchy was the degree of danger presented to children in these activities and the degree of responsiveness of the mother in attending to the needs of her children, either through responding herself or through obtaining help from others.

*Crime as a way to do mothering.* Women asserted that certain crimes did not conflict with being a good mother but instead supported it. For women whose criminal activity revolved around property crime, like shoplifting and fraud, or minor drug offenses, there seemed to be little conflict between motherhood and criminal activity. Most women suggested they shoplifted to increase family income and provide things for children impossible to obtain in any other way. As mothers who were their children's sole economic and physical support, gaining additional resources was considered by these mothers to be part of their responsibilities as caretakers. Randie, a mother of three children who was serving her first term, did not believe that good mothering conflicted with committing property crime.

> You can be a good mother and be involved in crime and shoplifting and stuff, but with drugs it's another thing.

Holly, a white woman in her thirties, became involved in drug trafficking, using the benefits to provide herself and her children a comfortable lifestyle.

> The dealer said think about all the money for you and the kids. They always loved my kids. I did the whole thing [managing a drug-selling operation] myself. That lasted quite a while.

Other inmate mothers found themselves in situations in which they saw opportunities and mandates to safeguard their children. Living in violence-prone communities and families pushed women to take active roles to protect their children. Women linked their responsibilities to safeguard children to the crimes that led them to incarceration. Susan and Inez both used violence to protect children against assault by others, defending their children even if this meant imprisonment.

> *Susan:* If you look at my record, you will see that I am in here for assault. But for me, I had to do that to protect my kids. No one else would take up that fight so I had to.

> *Inez:* They know I've did a little bit of everything for them. They seen me in action. They know that if they get into a fight and lost, I would beat that person up. I love them.

Although some would contend that good mothers should not resort to violence to resolve disputes involving their children, Susan and Inez justified using force as a strategy to protect their children when they thought they were in danger.

*Successfully balancing motherhood and drugs.* Although balancing drug use and motherhood became a challenge for some women, drug use was not necessarily antithetical to motherhood any more than other forms of recreation and relaxation. Many women believed it was possible to take drugs and maintain mothering responsibilities. A conversation with Stacy illustrates how women managed motherhood and drug use.

> *Stacy:* I had a perfectly normal life. I would get up in morning, get my son ready for school, get him on the bus, go to work, pick him up, feed him, and put him to bed. Then after, I would do what I need to do [to get high].
> *Enos:* So, you managed to *combine* being a mother and being an addict.
> *Stacy:* No, that's not it at all. I didn't *combine* those two things. I kept them completely *separate*.

Separating mother and drug-user identities was facilitated by drawing time limits around each. The use of drugs did not threaten the performance of mothering because it was confined to a time when mothers were off the "mother schedule" and the daily work of mothering was accomplished. The management of duties associated with good mothering was performed by this inmate mother, although some would allege that maintaining such a balancing act cannot not be successful in the long run. Other inmate mothers maintained that even in the short term, use of illegal substances undermined a mother's ability to judge whether she was a "good mother."

While inmate mothers maintained they were performing the mothering role by completing mothering tasks, other women distinguished between *thinking* one is doing good mothering and actually *doing* good mothering. Tee, a woman with several incarcerations and a drug habit, distinguished between committing crimes and/or taking drugs and the consequences of those behaviors for the future, especially in the event that the lawbreaking activity led to incarceration.

> You think you're doing right, but you're really not. You are doing so many things, but you really don't know what you're doing really. You think you're being good, but you're not. You're neglecting them because you're taking a chance by going stealing and risking yourself. You might not come back to them knowing that they love you.

*Compromising motherhood.* Although a number of women stated that it was possible to separate addiction and criminality from mothering, Irene, an episodic user of drugs, contended that it was not a long-term proposition.

> You can be an addict and a mother for a while. You can go along for just so long and then eventually something will go out of control.

Others also argued that it was impossible to separate addiction and motherhood. Margaret and Maya explained that drug addiction was a constant presence in their lives as mothers. Neither children nor drugs could be denied; both were demanding and needed attention.

> *Margaret:* Can't nobody say they didn't do it [take drugs] in front of their kids, because they're lying. That addiction is always there.
>
> *Maya:* Heroin is like a child that you will always carry with you until you stop or want to get help.

The out-of-control nature of their addictions was what these women identified as leading to their conclusion that it was impossible to separate addiction and motherhood. Margaret and April, both heavy users of drugs, described how powerful addictions eventually involved children, increasingly exposing them to seeing their mothers secure and ingest drugs.

> *Margaret:* Pretty soon, the kid is coming on your missions. You are taking them to the crack house. Pretty soon, everything in your house is gone because you are selling everything in it.
>
> *April:* I would take my son when he was a baby with me [to smoke cocaine]. I would lay him on the bed when I was getting high and my friends would be saying, "Hey, your baby is crying," and I would say, "Just a minute. Let me finish."

At a critical point in the struggle to balance addiction and motherhood, women became aware that their behavior was affecting their children. Other priorities, like getting high and supporting a habit, had replaced their children as a focus of their attention. Although some women contended that they successfully hid their use of drugs and work on the streets from their children, others reported that their children were very aware of their activities and attempted to manage their habits by hiding drugs, interfering in drug sales, and using other strategies.

*Children and drugs.* For a few women who were engaged in using and selling drugs, children became involved as "helpers." Younger children were employed as assistants, sometimes in minor roles, and served as lookouts when drugs were being sold out of their home. Older children were also involved in drug sales and used the mother's contacts to become moderately successful in the drug-dealing business. Early in her career, Inez's children tried to correct or influence her drug usage. Like many serious drug users, this woman was convinced that even very young children know when their mothers are using drugs and will attempt to influence their mother's behavior.

> My baby was two years old and he would sit outside the door, kick it, and cry because he knew I was getting high. He would kick and kick and kick. Then I would come out and he would go, "Oh" [sigh of relief], and he would be smiling.

In some instances, older children resisted the involvement of their mothers in drugs and crime by exerting whatever control they could. An older son who was not involved in drug sales had recently tried to curb his mother's drug use by threatening his mother's supplier with violence.

> He would say, "Anybody sell my mother drugs, I will shoot them in the leg."

Other children in this woman's family were involved in the drug trade.

*Using other resources to manage motherhood.* In some instances women found they were unable to both provide for children and engage in drug use and crime, and they appealed to others for help. Committed to a lifestyle that involved drugs and crime, inmate mothers had either lost custody of their children to strangers or relied on family and husbands for child care. Nicole suggested that resources were available so that children need not suffer when mothers were using drugs.

> I've done drugs but I've always had food. And if I didn't have enough money or if I was sick, I would call my mother and say, "Can you bring me some food? Can you please help me?"

The uncontrollable nature of drug addiction meant that women would find themselves in situations where their own resources for mothering were depleted. In these instances, arrangements could be made to protect the child(ren) from the mother's inability to provide care. As April noted, steps had to be taken to care for children when she was under the influence of some drugs.

> You know what? I never put them in jeopardy when I was on the streets. I did drugs. Yes, I did. But at that time, I wasn't into heroin. I was doing a little coke, snorting it. Nothing to make me drowsy or anything. Just to make me very hyper where I'd pay attention to them. I would feed them and do my motherly thing. Then when they went to bed, I would snort. When you're doing coke, you're always alert. So if something was to happen, I would be right on it. With heroin, it's a down. It's like Valium, you got to sleep. That's when I got into that, I said, "Mom please, you got to take these kids." Because if something were to happen to them, I would really kill myself.

One strategy for managing drugs, crime, and children was to have others take care of children when a woman was "on a mission." Alice, anticipating a drug raid, moved her children to her mother's house so they would not see her being arrested and so they would not be in danger.

> I was involved with drugs. When I knew the cops were coming, I moved my kids to my mom's house. My house was full of drugs.

Other women placed children with caretakers for longer periods of time, as noted above. The availability of these options was greater in situations where the drug use of the woman was known and recognized by partners, relatives, and others. In situations where the needs for placement of children were frequent and for long periods of time, women had to account for their absences. In these situations, mothers suspended their mothering for a period of time till they and others felt they were capable of resuming care for their children. These arrangements were described by Inez and Irene.

> *Inez:* As long as I'm not on drugs, they see I'm doing good, they'll give them to me. Which they don't have to do anyway, because as soon as I'm out, my kids come right to me anyway.

> *Irene:* The agreement I have with my mom says until I am ready to take care of him, she'll take care of him.

Taking a leave from the care of children supported women's identities as mothers, because responsibility for child care was transferred. Transferring responsibility for child care when a mother was not able to take care of children because of crime and drug problems was similar to arranging care when a mother was ill and poorly equipped for child care. Leaving children in one's care when one was sick placed them at risk for neglect. Bad mothering in this situation was claiming the right to take care of children when one was clearly incapable of exercising good motherly care. However, transferring responsibility was not cost-free. Assigning care to others might encourage caretakers to put mothers in peripheral roles and positions with respect to their children. Caretakers who were concerned about continuity of care for children and the unpredictable nature of the mother's addiction and criminal lifestyle took measures to protect their roles and positions with respect to children as well. The longer caretakers performed central roles in the lives of children of inmate mothers, the more likely it was that mothers would lose place and position vis-à-vis their children.

Although inmate mothers struggled to maintain positions and roles with respect to children, there were instances where their failures to perform as mothers were evident. Their failures at mothering could be attributed to multiple causes. If an inmate mother had few resources to rely on for good-quality care for children in her absence, there was a strong likelihood that she would lose battles over children and accept identity as a failed mother. This was especially the case when other providers were interested in her children and when family resources were depleted. Typically, mothers linked loss of children to the use of drugs.

*Losing the battle.* Women suggested that when they were addicted, drugs became their central focus, overriding all other concerns.

> *Belinda:* Some women say "Yes, you can be an addict and a mother," but overall to be honest with you. No. The drug overcomes the parent, because that's why my kids are where they are at now.

> *Margaret:* I see myself going downward because of drugs. It messed up the kids, because I still wanted the drugs more than I wanted my kids' lives. That bothers me a lot. That's a real hurting thing. . . . So I can't say that I didn't shoot up or bring them to the coke house. I did it all right in front of my kids and everything—the worst things.

This acceptance of the label of poor mother when under the influence of drugs bracketed poor motherhood and left open the possibility of good mothering under other circumstances—that is to say, when one was sober. Inmate mothers saw the loss of children through the termination of parental rights as punishment for failures, mainly tied to drug use. In instances where the rights to children were to be legally terminated by the child-welfare agency, women had to reconcile themselves to the loss. Lonnie explained that losing children to child welfare might be unavoidable.

> Even if they take my kids away, I know in my heart that I did everything I could.

Inmate mothers' acceptance of the loss of children eventually became a matter of understanding that it was impossible to regain lost ground with respect to rights to children. In cases like Lonnie's where her child had been placed in foster care soon after his birth and remained there during her two-year incarceration, reclaiming children was an uphill battle. Inmate mothers found that having foster parents interested in children indicated that they would be taken care of, but it might also mean that she would lose in a future contest over children.

SUMMARY

Balancing work as addicts and criminals with motherhood presented inmate mothers with an array of difficult situations. The hierarchy of motherhood, drug use and criminality suggested by inmate mothers provides a notion of how these women constructed motherhood under significant strain. This hierarchy also indicates that while some women claimed that dual identities could be maintained, this was not a long-term prospect. Inmate mothers contended that the chronic use of drugs would overcome the mother, resulting in her failure to perform mothering tasks. For some women, getting clean and sober enough to recognize that others were better able to take care of her children was a significant step in leaving behind identities as addicts and criminals. On the other hand, some inmate mothers maintained mother identity even if they lacked legal standing to make these claims. Finally, for some women, identities as mothers and as criminal and addicts were managed and negotiated with caretakers. Mothers and caretakers moved in and out of central caretaking positions in the lives of children. It appeared that the assistance and support of other caretakers were essential if women were to maintain this balance.

The next chapter, which synthesizes the findings from this research, examines how the social situations that faced inmate mothers varied according to the differences in the population behind bars. These differences have implications for careers as mothers and for the development of policies on the part of correctional agencies, child welfare, and those doing research in this area, as well.

Chapter 6

# Conclusions and Recommendations

The aim of this study has been to understand how women construct and manage motherhood in prison. This research project was responsive to a number of issues raised by scholars in the fields of family, women and crime, and motherhood and mothering. First, the lack of research on women offenders has been noted by many in the fields of deviance and criminal justice (Daly and Chesney-Lind 1988; Schur 1983; Smart 1976). By focusing on women in prison, this project has put women at the center of the analysis. This does not usually occur in studies that involve the criminal justice system, and, specifically, corrections. Second, research that accounts for how race and ethnicity presents and structures different opportunities and meanings around experience is also limited. This study has examined how race and ethnicity affect the way inmate mothers confront and manage challenges to arranging child care for their children. Third, many scholars have pointed to the need for research that carefully and closely examines what is entailed by positions, roles, and practices associated with mothering and motherhood. By investigating how motherhood is managed when mothers are apart from their children, this research has explored differences between being a mother, doing mothering, and maintaining position as a mother while in prison. Finally, scholars have also suggested that investigations of motherhood and mothering must include women who are not typical subjects of this research. To understand motherhood, researchers must incorporate not only white middle-class women in their studies, but must include mothers who are doing motherhood under severe stress and with limited resources. Our examination of mothers in these situations has revealed important dynamics of family responses that would not have occurred in more routine interactions.

Incarceration presented mothers with the difficult task of maintaining their identities, positions, and roles as mothers in families. This analysis has provided a rich understanding of how relations with family and caretakers and paths to prison affected where children lived while mothers were in prison. It has also examined how inmate mothers demonstrated fitness; negotiated for children; and balanced criminality, addiction, and motherhood while fashioning and constructing mother roles and positions with respect to children and others. Because the population of women inmates was quite varied, inmate mothers faced a variety of situational contingencies. These were important in that they presented individual inmate mothers with distinct challenges as they attempted to manage motherhood. These dimensions included the age of children, the involvement of child welfare, the length of the woman's sentence, her status as recidivist, and the living arrangement of children prior to the incarceration of the mother. In this research, I have determined that race and ethnicity do have important effects on situational contingencies and the responses to them. The racial and ethnic backgrounds of women inmates provided them with cultural and social resources with which to construct and reflect upon the work they did as mothers within and apart from their families. In the following discussion, I will outline the major findings of this research and discuss how mother careers have emerged in this setting.

FINDINGS

• The differential use of living arrangements for children reflected differences in the understandings of family obligations that appeared to have cultural and structural origins. The more frequent use of foster care and husbands by white inmate mothers appears to be related to how the white women evaluated the likelihood and desirability of relying on families of origin for assistance with child care. Black and Hispanic women, who typically relied on family for caretaking of children, considered family to be both available and optimal for child care. Differential use of living arrangements rested upon expectations of what families did for members in the situation of imprisonment.

- Whether families responded positively to the crisis of incarceration of an inmate mother depended upon the mother's determination of cost and benefit of that help as well as the family's assessment of whether the crisis could be handled without damage to the family itself. White inmate mothers appeared to be less likely to rely on family because of anticipated costs of the assistance and a negative assessment of their families. Families of African American and Hispanic women were more likely to offer assistance with children and inmate mothers were less likely to be estranged from them prior to incarceration.

- Paths to prison distinguished white, African American, and Hispanic women. Typically, white women entered criminal lifestyles by virtue of running away from home, African Americans through domestic networks, and Hispanic women through drug abuse. These routes were somewhat connected to how inmate mothers accessed the various options for placements of their children. White women were more likely to be alienated from their families and less likely to rely on family resources. African American and Hispanic women were unlikely to be distanced from their families and made greater use of these resources. In instances where white women were recruited to criminal lifestyles through domestic networks, they were less likely to be estranged from family and more likely to rely on family for assistance. This may reflect patterns of "expectations of troubles" in families that are marginalized and have repeated encounters with formal systems of social control and social services. Such families may develop mechanisms to respond to members' involvement with these agencies; typically, they do not work to expel these members, but to accommodate member absence or failure. "Expectations of trouble" were seen in all racial and ethnic groups.

- African American and Hispanic families appeared more likely to extend help in times of crisis unless family resources were depleted. For white women, the availability of family resources did not necessarily mean family extension during crisis in the manner that it did for women of color, except for those white families with expectations of troubles.

- Although white women traced the sources of their paths to prison to poor parenting, few African American or Hispanic women made this link. This difference in attributions created or constrained placement options for children.

- The quality of relationships between inmate mothers and caretakers determined the trajectory of mothers' roles and relationships with respect to children. Women with supportive and competent caretakers for their children were more likely to maintain positions and roles in the lives of their children. The positions and roles of mothers who faced hostile or incompetent caretakers were jeopardized as others with interests in the children moved into or attempted to undermine the mothers' place with respect to their children. Overall, white families appeared less supportive of inmate mothers with respect to children than African American and Hispanic families. They seemed to be more flexible and more willing to take on children without the mother's incurring any long-term debt with respect to family members.

- A variety of claims were made to motherhood. These rested on biology, experience with caretaking, and the uniqueness of the mother-child relationship. Because inmate mothers were separated from children, an array of actions, positions, and relationships emerged among mothers, children, and caretakers that highlighted the complexity of the mother role, position, and performance. Tasks and work associated with mothering were typically redistributed to caretakers and children in the mother's absence. Frequently, inmate mothers reported that much of the work that is done by mothers was left undone during their incarceration.

- Demonstrating fitness to official agencies (child welfare and corrections) and to interested others was accomplished through actions and through identity talk. Actions included enrollment in programs, planning for reunification, and other displays. To maintain identities as mothers, inmates employed a variety of defensive strategies, including bracketing (separating the past from the present) and distancing (separating self from other inmates and from "bad mothers").

- Children served as resources in a variety of ways. Because of the importance of children in identity work, the loss of children through termination of rights carried enormous weight. It is important to note, however, that legal status does not reflect in total the nature or quality of relationships among mothers, children, or caretakers. Some families develop informal systems of social control that are in some ways parallel to those of child-welfare agencies in their control of access to children and in assessment and attempts to manage mother behavior. Contests over children were more likely when caretakers were not supportive and when mothers had failed on a number of occasions to provide care for their children that was satisfactory to interested others. Black women and Hispanic women appeared to be more likely to share ownership of children with other caretakers than were white women. In white families, children were more likely to be considered as caretaking burdens and less likely to be regarded as community and family resources.

- As women faced the predicament of being mothers and criminals and/or addicts, they attempted to perform roles as mothers in a variety of ways. Some mothers saw their crimes as supporting and responding to the needs of their families. In these instances, women saw little conflict between their behavior and being a good mother. In other instances, being a good mother and an addict meant assigning others care of children, at least for the periods when mothers recognized that motherhood was not the identity that was most salient. One key measure of "good mothering" was knowing when one was not being a "good mother" and when plans needed to be made to find a substitute caregiver.

- Women were able to balance identities and work as mothers, addicts, and criminals under certain situations. However, as habits became serious or as criminality grew, inmate mothers had to confront changed circumstances and assign others caretaking, thereby becoming less involved with children. In some instances, women with serious drug involvement were pushed by caretakers or child welfare to terminate relationships with children.

CAREERS AS MOTHERS

Our findings show important variations among inmate mothers. These differences reflect relationships and dimensions (age of children, recidivism experience, length of sentence, and so on) that preceded incarceration and produced outcomes for women with respect to their careers as mothers and as addicts and criminals. As mothers in prison attempted to arrange and manage child care, do mothering, demonstrate fitness, negotiate over children, and balance crime, drugs, and motherhood, the differences between women became especially evident. These situational contingencies, taken together with the dimensions, combined to create four different mother trajectories. These trajectories illuminate the development of inmate mother careers and suggest that these paths were contingent upon a complex set of factors. These trajectories trace mothering and motherhood careers, and demonstrate how commitment and attachment to motherhood took distinct paths as women encountered challenges to motherhood before, during, and after incarceration. These trajectories are shown in figure 1 and are outlined below.

MOTHERHOOD TRAJECTORIES

*Trajectory A: Motherhood accepted.* Women in this trajectory had early entry to crime and life on the streets and had children taken care of by others. Without major responsibility for children prior to incarceration, five inmate mothers were assuming tasks associated with mothering with plans to move into positions as mother-caretakers of their children upon release, positions previously occupied by others in the mother's stead. For these women, the salience of mother identity was perhaps as great as it had ever been, and this provided incentive for changing behaviors related to crime and drug use. As seen in figure 1, performance as a mother and commitment to motherhood was low prior to incarceration and increased during incarceration.

*Trajectory B: Motherhood terminated.* Four inmate mothers with serious drug involvement and depleted family resources either had lost children to child welfare or were about to lose children to adoption. The termination of parental rights often followed a trajectory of decreasing involvement with children and caretakers. As shown in figure 1, the mothers were previously involved with children, but this caretaking declined with repeated incarcerations, leading to legal severance of rights to children. This trajectory was also followed by mothers

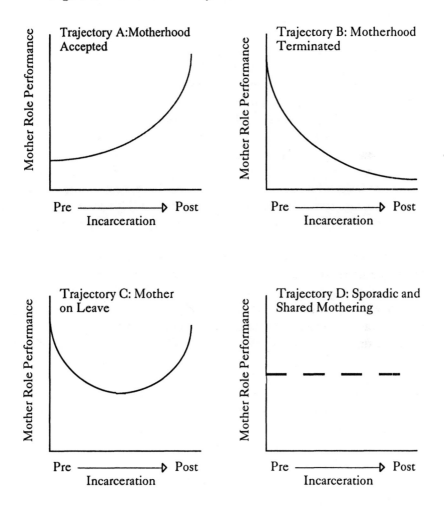

Figure 1. Mother Career Trajectories

whose children had been adopted by other relatives. In this case, mothers had removed themselves from mothering particular children and were focusing on improving their relationships with respect to other children. The salience of mother identity was tied to "new" children and the loss of others was bracketed.

*Trajectory C: Mother on leave.* This mother trajectory reflected the experience of nine women who had minimal exposure to and involvement with crime, addiction, and the streets before incarceration. Caretakers supervising their children were supportive and did not intend to undermine or undercut the role and position of mothers in the family. Mothers' involvement in the lives of their children, which was extensive and central prior to incarceration, would most likely resume after release from prison. In a few instances, caretakers were incompetent or hostile and return of children to the mother's care might become complicated by battles over ownership. However, because these inmate mothers were committed to motherhood, they were likely to mount a struggle to regain custody of children. The "mother on leave" trajectory shows a decline in mother performance due to incarceration and a resumption of motherhood at the end of imprisonment.

*Trajectory D: Shared or sporadic mothering.* In "sporadic" or "shared" mothering, seven mothers shared caretaking with others or moved in and out of mother positions with respect to children. For mothers with significant involvement in crime, drugs, and life on the street, relationships with children were mediated by other caretakers. In these arrangements, children had been taken care of by others prior to the incarceration of the inmate mother. Because mothers were not primary caretakers prior to incarceration, typically children did not suffer disruption in living arrangements. Involvement with the children was somewhat sporadic when inmate mothers were in the community, and this could remain the case upon release. The importance of supportive and competent caretakers was essential to enable the inmate mother to continue her work as a criminal or addict and mother. The salience of mother identity did not have an impact here as a possible deterrent to crime and addiction. This trajectory showed minimal or moderate involvement with children before, during, and after incarceration.

## CONCLUSIONS AND RECOMMENDATIONS

Differences in the inmate populations in terms of characteristics and in terms of mothering trajectories have important implications for policy and program development. Seven major conclusions are discussed below with accompanying recommendations for these. Although the sample of women interviewed was small, I maintain that these conclusions can be generalized to inmate mothers in other jurisdictions.

*Conclusion 1: Racial and ethnic differences between inmate mothers have significant impacts on the living arrangements of children.*

Race and ethnicity make a difference in how caretaking is arranged and provided for children of inmate mothers. The resources available to inmate mothers for child keeping vary across families. Family elasticity also varies across race, class, and ethnicity. It is apparent in this research that inmate mothers come to prison with a wide range of resources at their disposal. While some women enter correctional institutions with intact families and supportive relationships, many do not. Although some are able to rely on family and kin for the care of their children, these caretakers are often placed under significant economic and emotional stress in attempting to provide homes for these children. While some women are able to rely on the child welfare system to provide child care, these arrangements also carry serious implications for the child and the mother in terms of legal involvement, challenges to custody, and related issues.

The ability of the family to survive and respond to the crises brought about by the incarceration of a female member is strongly affected by where the family is located in the social and economic structure. It appears that given the sort of family crises discussed here, families with lower social status and fewer economic resources are more flexible in responding to these situations. A family's understanding of whether responding to the crises will endanger the family is a major factor here. Family elasticity needs to be examined not just in accommodating additional members in households but in the ability of the family and its members to respond to a number of different crises. Inmate mothers' understandings of how families of different races and ethnicities respond to the incarceration of women provide insights into how families come to be obligated to members.

As noted in earlier research, few African American and Hispanic mothers avail themselves of foster care for children. It is not that these services are not offered or available to families of color, but these inmate mothers are not confident that their children will receive good care in the foster-care system. Foster care appears to be the last resort for children of color and is not used unless all family resources are depleted. From the perspective of an overburdened child-welfare system, this reliance upon family to care for children is most likely welcomed. However, this is often interpreted by state workers and agency staff to indicate that these families will "take care of their own" (Billingsley and Giovannoni 1972; Solinger 1992), leaving some families willing to care for children but seriously strapped in terms of financial, emotional, and other resources.

Race and ethnicity also appear to make a difference with respect to claims to children and ownership. Black women and Hispanic women appear to be more likely to share ownership of children with other caretakers than are white women. As previously mentioned, in white families children are more likely to be considered as caretaking burdens and less likely to be regarded as community and family resources. These differences are also reflected in the ways families rely on formal and informal systems of social control to influence, control, and intervene in the lives of inmate mothers.

*Recommendation: Racial and ethnic differences should be recognized in programming and policy making.*

Because race and ethnicity are related in these situations to family support of children and mothers, attention should be paid to evaluating the resources that families provide for children. Support of families and other caretakers during incarceration and after the mother's release could provide important interventions that might avoid future displacement of children. Programs need to take advantage of the strengths of family structure and be sensitive to how informal systems of child care may be very effective in controlling the behavior of mothers who are seriously crime- and drug-involved.

Some programs have been developed to address the needs of inmate mothers and their children (Stuart 1997). These programs vary in both their stated objectives and their focus. Some aim to enhance the likelihood that mother and child will be reunited after incarceration. Others focus on providing extended visitation, reducing the substance dependency of inmate mothers, delivering parenting education, and providing legal advocacy in custody matters. These programs should attend to the variety of family forms that inmate mothers bring to prison and accommodate these differences.

*Conclusion 2: Inmate mothers vary in the level and quality of family and other resources at their disposal to assure good care for children.*

Families provide resources and support for some inmate mothers. However, it is important to note that some of these families have also provided pathways to crime and drug use for these women. Returning to these homes may make successful reintegration into the community unlikely. In some instances, inmate mothers are estranged from their families and rely on husbands, boyfriends, and foster care for their children. However, independent of who is taking care of children, inmate mothers have little power to influence and monitor the care being given to children. Resources that might assist an inmate mother to arrange and manage good care for children appear to be inadequate. If the mother's case is not known to child welfare, enlisting the assistance of this agency often jeopardizes the mother's relationship to her children by promoting an investigation.

*Recommendation: Mothers and children need a variety of services, as do caretakers. Seeking help in family crises should not be tied to opening investigations of the family.*

Attention should be paid to how families can obtain assistance from child welfare and other agencies without putting the family into legal jeopardy (Washington 1988). These programs become increasingly important as the population of women in prison continues to grow, as networks of family support that used to characterize communities of color may be weakening and deteriorating (Collins 1990; Roschelle 1997), and as rules and regulations set forth by the federal

Adoption and Safe Families Act of 1997 speed up the processes by which children are freed for adoption.

*Conclusion 3: While in prison, inmate mothers are under considerable pressure to demonstrate fitness as mothers. Failure to demonstrate fitness has serious implications for their future with their children, especially if the case is active with child welfare. Because of the increasing population of inmate mothers behind bars, the numbers of children affected will likely increase in the future.*

Some argue that the basis of sentencing and child-welfare policies rests on stereotyped ideas about "bad mothers" and the need to separate "unfit mothers" from their children (Golden 1997). Inmate mothers with serious drug problems and sometimes even those with minor criminal offenses face overwhelming odds in reuniting with children. Because of low social margin, failure in one area may mean failure in attempts to reengage mothering. For example, although inmate mothers may be interested in drug-treatment programs after release, they may be pushed to live with children to demonstrate their acceptance of child-care responsibilities. Not being involved in treatment may be interpreted as a lack of commitment to changing lifestyles that endanger performance as a mother; at the same time, enrolling in residential programs may delay mothers' taking on of responsibility for the care of children. These dilemmas confront inmate mothers who have multiple problems and few resources to deal with them.

As this research shows, women who are attempting to regain or maintain legal custody of their children face significant institutional obstacles in demonstrating fitness for motherhood. Holding inmate mothers to standards of performance that are difficult for mothers in the community to meet doubly punishes women by using their term of imprisonment as evidence that they are unfit mothers (Beckerman 1994). Also, child-welfare policies that minimize the use of long-term foster care may push courts to terminate parental rights, not because an inmate is an unfit mother, but because she is an absent parent and lacks resources to demonstrate an ability to care for children (Beckerman 1991).

*Recommendation: Child welfare and correctional staff need to be aware of the obstacles faced by inmate mothers in demonstrating fitness in institutional contexts and more closely coordinate case and discharge planning efforts.*

Providing good care for children while their mothers are incarcerated is essential. Balancing the needs of children for safe, secure, and good care with the inmate mother's timetable for returning or adopting motherhood is never a simple matter. Child welfare and correctional staff need to work more closely together to coordinate case planning, especially for women whose relationships to children are problematic. Advocacy for inmate mothers on child-custody issues needs to be developed and incorporated into other treatment programs (Johnston 1995b). Some women who are unable to care for their children because of chronic drug abuse resist efforts by child welfare to terminate their parental rights. In some cases, this resistance rests on a fear that they will never see their children again. To address these concerns, some jurisdictions are availing themselves of open adoptions. These adoptions support and, in some cases, promote contact between the mother and her adopted children. This provides some mothers with the knowledge that they can establish a relationship with their children even though legal proceedings have terminated parental rights.

*Conclusion 4: Not all inmate mothers will be long-term caretakers of children.*

As other researchers have noted and as this research indicates, relationships between incarcerated women and their children vary widely, resulting in a variety of inmate mother careers. The majority of inmate mothers expressed a wish to live with children after incarceration. However, for many this desire is based more on an unrealistic understanding of the demands of child care than on a careful evaluation of what they are able to provide for their children. While there are exceptions, most inmate mothers face enormous stresses upon release, placing them in high-risk situations with respect to children (Koban 1985). Research has demonstrated that for certain inmates, successful reunification with children is unlikely. These inmates are characterized by histories of substance abuse, prior incarcerations, and lengthy sentences (Fessler 1991). Each of these factors has compromised the ability of inmate mothers to develop and maintain relationships with children. While many of these mothers will be reunited with their children and provide stable homes for them, others will not.

Approximately one-third of the mothers will not reunite with children or take on major responsibility for child care (Martin 1997). Despite mothers' verbal commitments to be involved in the lives of their children, some inmate mothers are not able to be good or even adequate mothers to these particular children at this point in their lives.

> [I]t is important not to romanticize the mother-child bond and ignore the reality that some other mothers are not capable of adequate parenting. Aggressive intervention for children whose mothers are chronically chemically dependent, neglectful, abusive, and engage in repeated criminal activity must protect the children of the minority of mothers who are inadequate parents. (Martin 1997, 21)

It is likely that inmate mothers' persistence in lives of crime and drug abuse will open up opportunities for other caretakers to provide care for children, with support from other family members and perhaps the state.

*Recommendation: Correctional staff and others involved in programming should develop ways to recognize "promising" and "problem" mothers as early as possible in inmate mother careers.*

Research suggests profiles that can be employed by agency staff to identify mothers who are unlikely to reunify with children. Programs should acknowledge the intractability of serious drug abuse and provide early intervention for these inmate mothers. As discovered here, inmate mothers follow a number of inmate mother trajectories. These are important to consider in program design and interventions. The relevance of these will be addressed below.

*Conclusion 5: Children of incarcerated mothers face significant disruptions in living arrangements.*

Reports on the population of incarcerated mothers document the level of disruption faced by the children of inmate mothers in terms of changes of living arrangements, caretakers, and schools. Disruption is especially serious when inmate mothers are providing child care prior to incarceration. For many women who are sentenced to prison, incarceration appears not to be an appropriate punishment. This is especially the case for women who present minimal danger to communities and whose criminal records do not require that they be confined to a correctional facility (Bloom and Steinhart 1993; Chesney-Lind 1997).

*Recommendations: Alternatives to incarceration can divert many female offenders from incarceration and save children the pain of removal of parents from their homes.*

Experts estimate that the majority of women serving sentences behind bars could be diverted to community-based corrections without any increased danger to the community and at significantly lower costs (Immarigeon 1995). Correctional advocates have argued for years that community-based alternatives to imprisonment are more appropriate than incarceration for this population (American Correctional Association 1990; Chesney-Lind 1993). Some residential programs offer women community-based housing that accommodates children and serves as an alternative to imprisonment for women who pose few security risks (Blinn 1997). Alternative sentencing programs in which women remain in the community with their children would mitigate some of the damage to mother-child relationships that arises from incarceration.

*Conclusion 6: Women criminals are enmeshed in family networks of crime and as such may face more difficulty in maintaining crime- and drug-free lifestyles.*

Female inmates who have entered lives of drug dependence and crime through domestic networks face considerable challenges in leaving deviant lifestyles. For many inmate mothers, return to the community means reestablishment in environments that precipitated entry into crime and substance abuse in the first place. Although these domestic networks may be willing to provide care for children while women are in the community and during incarceration, it is important to recognize that these networks may be seriously overwhelmed by demands for care and support from other family members as well.

*Recommendation: The availability, willingness, and ability of caretakers to take care of children should be carefully assessed, with an accompanying development of caretaker supports to assure that children receive adequate services.*

Because children reside in a variety of living arrangements, the needs of caretakers are likely to be varied as well. Little attention is paid to the needs of these caretakers for emotional, financial, and legal assistance. Although some families are taking care of children with minimal need for outside assistance, the resources of others are seriously strained. Some relative and kin care can be inadequate for children simply because caretakers are overburdened. As a recent report noted, because some relative caretakers are overwhelmed by demands from other family members, foster homes proved to be better settings for children (Gaudin and Sutphen 1993).

*Conclusion 7: The career trajectories of inmate mothers vary considerably and these have serious implications for creating appropriate program interventions.*

How women manage motherhood in prison is often a result of factors and dimensions that have preceded incarceration. Managing motherhood is also dependent upon the strategies taken to confront the challenges that face women as they serve time in prison. The four careers identified in this research—motherhood accepted, motherhood terminated, mother on leave, and suspended mothering—reflect important differences between inmate mothers in their relationships with caretakers and their children, their enactment of and commitment to the mother role and position, and their likelihood of reunification with their children as primary caregivers.

Most inmate mothers will live with their children after release. For some, incarceration means an interruption in mothering but not does signal a deterioration in the relationship among children, mothers, and caretakers. Mothers will resume the mothering they did prior to incarceration. For other mothers, incarceration provides an incentive to reunify with children, because other caretakers have issued an ultimatum that no future care will be provided after incarceration. These inmate mothers have never taken responsibility for child care and must accept and adapt to mothering after incarceration. Although both mothers will move into mothering roles after release, they face that role with different experiences. Other inmates will not take up major responsibility for child care after release. Some will have their parental rights terminated, while others will share child care with others.

*Recommendation: Because these trajectories reflect distinct careers with respect to the care of children, attention should be given to creating interventions that are appropriate to inmate mothers' needs for assistance.*

For example, for women whose mothering is suspended during incarceration, attention should be directed to maintaining contact and involvement with children and helping the family to deal with the trauma of incarceration. Women who will be taking on child-care responsibility for the first time will require more intensive parenting skills and case planning for reunification. In the case of women whose parental rights will be terminated, child welfare and correctional staff can provide better communication about the case to the inmate mother. Open adoption alternatives can be explored, as noted above.

### SUMMARY

This research has provided a detailed examination of how women manage motherhood in prison and how this differs for white women and women of color. According to Hammersley (1990), ethnographic research should produce knowledge that is relevant. The relevance of this research rests on several bases. First, given an anticipated increase in the number of women who are incarcerated, we can expect growing numbers of children to be affected by the imprisonment of their mothers (DiMascio 1997). The development of a more comprehensive picture of the challenging situations women face in arranging and managing care for their children while incarcerated may help policy makers respond better to the various needs women present in correctional environments (Belknap 1996). With research indicating that positive relationships with children and with family are important links to postrelease integration into the community (Hairston 1991; Martin 1997; Farrell 1998), administrators need to pay attention to and develop programs specifically addressing the distinct needs of women and their children. Second, this research makes a contribution to understanding how race and ethnicity present families with opportunities and constraints as they attempt to respond to family crises. These differences between families have important implications not only for the care of children during imprisonment but also for long-term relationships between mothers, caretakers, and children. Finally, paying attention to families and mothers that usually do not receive attention from scholars provides important insights into how race, ethnicity, and class intersect to support or undermine mothers and motherhood in contemporary society.

Afterword

# "You Know What I'm Sayin'?"

As noted in chapter 1, the number of women behind bars continues to climb. Although there are attempts by policy advocates to reduce the overuse of incarceration for low-level drug offenders and others (Chesney-Lind and Immarigeon 1995; Donziger 1996), there seems to be little relief in sight from the punitive criminal justice policies of the past decade. The impact of the incarceration boom has hit our nation's communities and its families hard. Since I began this study in 1992, the number of women behind bars has increased by almost 75 percent (Maguire and Pastore 1998; Gilliard 1999; Beck 2000). In conducting this research, the tragedy of over-incarceration became clear through conversations with inmate mothers, their children, and their caretakers. In this afterword, I will present the research methodology, discuss the challenges of doing research on mothering in prison, and suggest ways in which researchers can be sensitive to conducting investigations in settings like this one.

## AN OVERVIEW OF THE RESEARCH SETTING

To examine these questions, I conducted research at a women's correctional facility in the northeastern United States in 1992, 1993, and 1997. As of midyear 1999, this facility housed approximately 230 women, 60 awaiting trial and the balance sentenced women. This is the state's only correctional facility for female offenders. Unlike correctional institutions located in larger states, this unit was relatively accessible for inmate visitation and was located within twenty to thirty minutes driving distance from areas where their families resided. As of 30 June 1997, the characteristics of the inmate population were as follows: the median age of the population was thirty-two years for the sentenced population and twenty-eight years for the population awaiting trial; racially and ethnicly the population was 61 percent white, 30 percent African American, 8 percent Hispanic, and 1 percent Native American. Seventy-five percent of the women had children under the age of eighteen, and 50 percent had active involvement with the child-welfare authorities. Finally, of the sentenced population, 20 percent were serving time for crimes of violence, 40 percent for public order crimes, 24 percent for property crimes, and 16 percent for drug-related crimes. Sixty-three percent were serving sentences of less than one year, 21 percent were serving one to three years, 12 percent were serving between three and ten years, andthe balance of the population (3 percent) were serving over ten years and life sentences (Rhode Island Department of Corrections 1996, 1997).

In 1992 and 1993, field research and initial interviewing were conducted at a parenting program located and operated within the correctional facility. The aim of the fieldwork was to examine how the parenting program worked within the women's prison. Parenting programs are designed to enhance the parenting skills of inmate mothers and rest on the premise that maintaining contact between mothers and children will have positive benefits on the women's rehabilitation. During the period of the research, women in the program presented a generally low security risk.* At this facility, the parenting program featured group therapy sessions about parenting skills and the impact of substance abuse on parenting, along with extended visiting at a site approximately one mile away from the correctional facility. This program operated with few of the trappings associated with a correctional facility. Correctional officers were not in uniform. There were no searches of visitors, children, or bags. Inmate families were allowed to bring in food from home. Finally, there was plenty of room for toys and play, and for conversation and privacy between inmate mothers and their children.

---

*The program has since expanded considerably. Parenting classes are offered in several facilities. Also, at present, parenting classes are held separately from extended visitation. However, to gain access to the extended visiting program, women must complete the parenting course and receive a certificate.

## RESEARCH METHODOLOGY

Because this topic had received limited attention, I decided to undertake a qualitative analysis using grounded theory (Charmaz 1983) and dimensional analysis (Schatzman 1991). Field observation was conducted in the spring of 1992 and in the summer of 1993. Access to the site was granted by the administrator of the women's facility. Over the first twenty-week period, I spent every Saturday conducting fieldwork at the site from 9:30 A.M. to 2:00 P.M. While there, I attended parenting group meetings, spoke with women and children in attendance, played with children, and participated in group activities.

I adopted the role of participant as observer (Denzin 1989) at the site and informed inmates, staff, and others that I was a researcher and a program volunteer. Informal interviews with program staff, correctional staff, chaplains, foster parents, and other caregivers were also conducted. In the summer of 1993, I returned to the setting and attended parenting programs held on Thursday evenings and Saturdays for a twelve-week period.

This fieldwork generated extensive field notes, along with analytical and methodological memos. This laid the groundwork for more focused exploration of questions that surfaced in the first stage of the research. For example, in conversations with inmate mothers, it became apparent that living arrangements of children appeared to be connected to the race or ethnicity of the mothers, with African American children living with family members and whites with husbands or in foster care. When a review of the literature was later completed, I found that these patterns reflected national trends. Other racial and ethnic differences emerged as well. In responding to questions about how they got to prison, white women more often connected the source of their troubles to bad homes and bad parents, which they responded to by running away from home. Black women, on the other hand, attributed their entry and persistence in crime to their own life choices and did not identify their families as the root of their problems. Black women, as well, identified family members and friends of family as providing their early entry into crime and the "fast life." These reports from inmates confirmed Miller's (1986) analysis of paths to prison. It became apparent that important relationships existed among race and ethnicity, paths to prison, and the choice of living arrangements for children.

Interest in investigating these patterns and exceptions to them led me to pursue the second stage of the research. Because I became interested in how women managed motherhood and mother identity while incarcerated, the focus of the research moved from observation in the parenting program to a more in-depth exploration of mothering and motherhood that was impossible to pursue at the program site. The second source of data was intensive interviews done with twenty-five women away from the parenting program. A purposive sample with maximum variation was gathered, reflecting important differences within the population that affect motherhood and mothering (Lincoln and Guba 1985). Subjects included women who were involved with the child-welfare system and those who were not; women who were chronic offenders, minor offenders, and nonrecidivists; women who had young children or infants, and those with teenagers; women who were serving lengthy, midrange, and brief sentences; women who were living with and apart from their children prior to incarceration; and women who were serving sentences for crimes of violence, property crime, drug-related offenses, and public order offenses. Of special concern was putting together a sample of inmate mothers who were racially and ethnically diverse and whose children's placements reflected dominant patterns, along with those that were exceptions or negative cases (Katz 1983). Appendix A includes short profiles of the twenty-five women interviewed; appendix B shows race and ethnicity of inmate mothers, along with living arrangements of their children.

Women were identified as potential prospects for interviews and recruited by program staff and by the researcher. To be a candidate for the research, a woman had to have children under the age of eighteen, be serving a sentence, be available for the interview, and agree to review and sign the consent form. Of all the women approached for participation, one declined to be interviewed because of her participation in other ongoing research at the facility. Prior to each interview, I informed each respondent that our conversation was completely confidential and that I had no connection with, or influence on, the parole board, treatment or classification staff, child welfare, or other authorities. All signed consent forms. These interviews lasted from one to two and a half hours. All the names used in the research report were changed. In some instances, women chose their own pseudonyms.

The interview guideline included broadly phrased questions and prompts to elicit conversation. Initial interviews and fieldwork, along with a reading of the literature, provided the basis for these questions. Several items of information collected at the beginning of the interview were close-ended and demographic. These included inmate age, length of sentence, prior incarceration, and controlling offense; number, age, sex, and living arrangements of children; and involvement of the child-welfare agency. Other items were asked in an open-ended fashion, for example, "Can you tell me how you arranged for care of your children?," "How did you come to prison?," "Are there things that only mothers can do for their children?," "How do you manage to stay involved with the day-to-day management of your children?," and "Can women be addicts and mothers?"

In many cases, life stories told by women obviated my need to ask questions or to provide prompts. In several instances, I related stories and observations provided by other respondents to the women and asked for their responses. For example, one of the first women I interviewed detailed her daily schedule, showing how she maintained a conventional life for herself and her child in the community. She explained that it was not until later in the evening, after she had completed daily household and mothering chores, that she used cocaine. I remarked that it appeared that she was able to *combine* being an addict and being a mother. She quickly corrected my interpretation, stating that she did not *combine* motherhood and addiction, but instead kept them completely *separate*. Her conceptualization of separating mothering and addiction provided the basis of questions about this issue that I brought up in all subsequent interviews with inmate mothers. I rephrased the exchange with this inmate (maintaining confidentiality and anonymity), made it into a story, and asked for women's responses. Relating this story and others like it provided me with credibility and established the fact that I had an understanding of the situations faced by inmate mothers. These stories also created a platform for women to respond critically or supportively to what other women were saying and also provided an opportunity to draw a distinction between themselves and other inmate mothers or further articulate a point made earlier in the interview.

The interviews were tape-recorded where possible, with additional note taking during the interview to identify matters of special interest that needed to be explored further. Interviews were transcribed and coded. ResearchWare, a software program for qualitative research, was employed to facilitate coding. The transcribed interviews were read several times, employing analyses that were informed by theory, relevant research, and by fieldwork at the site. For example, as I was examining how inmate mothers spoke about arranging care for children, a number of codes emerged related to family obligations, elasticity and expectations about what family members should do for each other in times of crisis. Women who received help from their families and those who did not both accounted for family responses to their incarceration. These codes were merged into larger categories and analyzed in the context of race and ethnicity, living arrangements of children, and paths to prison to determine if there were patterns that distinguished inmate mothers from each other.

Inmate mothers enumerated tasks, positions, connections, and relationships that reflected a variety of understandings and interpretations about motherhood management. These codes were combined into larger categories that served as the basis for understanding the tasks that inmate mothers faced in managing motherhood while in prison. It was through the social situations—arranging and managing caretakers, demonstrating fitness and others—that emerged in the coding that important differences and similarities emerged among inmate mothers in the ways in which mother work and family work was done.

### CHALLENGES IN CONDUCTING RESEARCH IN A CORRECTIONAL SETTING

Perhaps the biggest challenge in conducting a project like this is the development of a basis for understanding by the researcher of the world occupied by inmate mothers. How one comes to know a world is influenced by both the lenses one uses to explore that world and by who the researcher is, on a number of dimensions and social positions, and as well, by the worldview and world that one is interested in knowing about. One may assume (incorrectly) that learning about motherhood is a simple task because, as social actors, we are familiar with mothers and mothering. That familiarity, of course, can breed ignorance and can deny the reality of what is. Doing motherhood is a complex matter, in that it is both constructed and influenced by large structural factors. How one does motherhood and mothering depends very much upon the resources, social position, cultural factors, and other factors that one brings to the role and task. Talk about motherhood and mothering is caught up in discourses that reflect and support, to some extent, dominant ideologies about "good mothering." On the other hand, talk about mothering also challenges these myths of mothering, however, and reveals the resistance of women and their support of alternative ways to getting mothering done.

Looking at how mothering is done while mothers are incarcerated brings to light a variety of mothering styles. They do not so much reflect individual personal choices about how a specific woman will decide to mother while in prison, but instead reflect how women in different social positions respond to the challenges brought about by incarceration. Learning about mothering in this setting required that I leave "suspended" what I thought I knew about mothering. Over a twenty-year period, I had worked in the fields of corrections and child welfare, and had served as an instructor in sociology, teaching courses in the field of family and crime and in the field of criminal justice.

I did not enter the setting understanding that, despite years of teaching and working in the area, my ideas about mothering and motherhood were quite undeveloped. And, of course, as a middle-aged women, I had also been exposed to "mothering" and motherhood during virtually all of my life. Despite all this "knowing" about the topic, I was still relatively unprepared to enter the research setting. One can attempt to be open to the field and leave preconceptions at the door. But sensitivity to the setting and its inhabitants is not a quality that one brings to a research project; it is one that is under constant construction. My definitions of who a mother was, what a mother did, who could mother, what and who constituted a family and others were rapidly and regularly thrown into disorder by virtue of my fieldwork in the parenting program. For example, in entering the parenting program, I came with definitions of mother and mothering that reflected mainstream sociological understanding—that is, that mothers (birth mothers) did mothering (were the caretakers of children). This conceptualization is both apt and incorrect at the same time. Like others who have examined mothers and mothering, I quickly discovered how complex the nature of mothering was. Because mothers needed to have children taken care of, they were in a position to try to reproduce mothering for children not in their care. This allowed me to examine how it is that women think about mothering and motherhood. As I conducted in-depth interviews with inmate mothers, I became aware of how the nature of mothering and motherhood was complicated and complex. What is a mother? What did it mean to be a good mother? What do mothers do? What had to be done to provide a child with good mothering while inmates were in prison? Are there things that are unique about what mothers do in caretaking? What accounted for the differences in mother-child relationships and involvement in mothering?

I also entered the site with working hypotheses about caring for children. In my reading of the literature about female prisoners, I found that many had experienced child abuse and neglect.* I assumed that because of these histories, few women would want to place their children in the care of family members. As I conducted this research, I learned that this also was both accurate and not accurate. It may have some resonance for some inmate mothers, but for fewer than I had expected.

Like all programs in institutional settings, there were a myriad of regulations about participation in the parenting program. Rules governing this program were established so that inmate mothers and their children would develop closer relationships and mothers would improve parenting skills. While the program set out seemingly clear guidelines that only children of mothers, not their nieces or nephews, could visit their mothers in the parenting program, there were several complications that surfaced here. Institutional rules about program eligibility and which children could visit the women brought into clear focus how the structures of family and child keeping varied significantly among inmate mothers. In some cases, inmate mothers had not and would not assume child-care responsibility for children they had

---

*A survey of state prison inmates reported that more than half of the female inmates (57.2 percent) experienced physical or sexual abuse before their incarceration. The comparable figure for males is 16.1 percent. While both groups experienced abuse as children, maltreatment extended into adulthood for women (Harlow 1999).

given birth to, but would take charge of nieces and nephews or their grandchildren. While program administrators struggled to make certain that no one was taking unfair advantage of these extended visiting privileges, inmate mothers struggled to explain their complicated and complex arrangements for child care. This was especially the case for women of color.

Finally, the issue of researcher place surfaced. How do researchers from worlds that are significantly different bridge the gaps between respondents and themselves? How could I, as a white female sociologist with a working-class background, be reasonably certain that I could come to understand what inmates were saying in these interviews? How could I be reasonably sure that I could say "Yes" when inmate mothers asked me, "You know what I'm sayin'?"

### "YOU KNOW WHAT I'M SAYIN'?"

As an increasing number of critics of mainstream methodologies have written, researchers need to consider some important questions when they are conducting research and interpreting the results (DeVault 1995; Fine 1998). One of these is most appropriate to address here, the issue of how I could come to "know" what inmate mothers were really saying in our interviews. In an insightful article, DeVault (1995) suggests that in institutional settings, researchers need to be sensitive to the issue of race as it is used in dialogue.

> [D]o I know enough to . . . understand and interpret? . . . How did my knowledge—and perhaps, more importantly, my ignorance—shape our interaction and then my reading of the interview data produced in our encounter ?(1995, 626)

In examining motherhood in prison, what were the challenges to insuring that I would be learning what I intended to, that I would come to understand the situations faced by inmate mothers? In research that relies upon interviewing, Taylor, Gilligan, and Sullivan (1995) ask, who is speaking and who is listening? As they suggest, stories about lives, accounts, are "produced interactively, depending not only on the questions of the interviewer and the experiences of the narrator, but also on the 'social location' of both" (1995, 14). What needs to be taken into consideration when we assess whether a researcher has gotten the story right?

I employed a variety of strategies, trying to get the story right. As stated above, these in-depth interviews lasted from one to two and a half hours. The open-ended nature of these conversations allowed inmate mothers leeway to guide the interview and to provide a narrative life story that included information about mothering and motherhood. It appeared that the interview process and approach allowed for inmate mothers to tell their "stories" in a variety of ways.

The focus of this study was to learn how inmate mothers constructed and managed motherhood while incarcerated, and it was important to insure that this information was obtained and interpreted accurately. Because the aim here was to gain the perspective of mothers in prison, their knowledge and interpretation of their situation constituted the basis for developing an understanding of the development of identity in this situation. Most of the women in the sample were highly articulate about the challenges of managing motherhood in prison and provided rich narratives about their experiences before and during incarceration in managing relationships with their children. During interviews, women discussed at varying lengths paths to prison, individual children, adjusting to incarceration, substance abuse, plans for the future, and other topics. I made no attempt to limit inmate conversations, but allowed inmate mothers to render a story of their lives as they wished to express it.

Because the focus of the study was motherhood, there could have been efforts by inmate mothers to convey an idealized presentation of self as "good mothers." They might hide their true feelings about motherhood and mothering, or discuss motherhood as a central concern when, in fact, other matters carried greater weight. Given conventional gender norms, most women are socialized to provide answers to questions about motherhood and mothering that present them in a good light. But I believe that during the course of the interviews, the women for the most part spoke frankly and honestly about their failures as parents, about their estrangement from families and children, and about their own responsibilities for incarceration and trouble with the law. These stories were in no way idealized portraits of women who conformed to dominant ideologies of perfect mothers or who attempted to present themselves as "good mothers." Rather, the women discussed candidly their problems and their successes in mothering, assessing the past and fashioning a developing sense of identity as mothers. Inmate mothers also positioned themselves in a variety of mother roles, suggesting that most were ready and eager to speak about their interpretation of mothering in this context. Because nothing related in the interview would help or harm their status with others, I believe most inmate mothers provided frank responses to interview questions and prompts.

Checking stories through comparisons provided a good test of both the plausibility of accounts and the plausibility of interpretative frameworks suggested by the women. Further, in a number of instances, inmate mothers' accounts and interpretations were checked with other inmate mothers' accounts and interpretations (Lincoln and Guba 1985). For instance, in explaining differences between the responses of white and African American families to a woman's incarceration, one African American inmate proposed that white families were less tolerant of girls who were traditionally expected to follow conventional paths to adulthood than were some African American families. Because of this lower tolerance level, white families would be less likely to help inmate mothers. She further suggested that African American families were better able to extend help to women in crisis because these families expected trouble on account of their social position and society's racism. This "theory" was checked against relevant literature and was also presented to white, Hispanic, and African American mothers to learn their responses to this interpretation of family differences and their implication for inmate mothers. This theorizing provided opportunities to develop and refine interpretative frameworks and also to gain a clearer understanding of how inmate mothers conceptualized differences between them in mothering and motherhood. It was clear that these expectations of trouble obtained for white and Hispanic families as well as for black families who were at the social margins. Asking inmate mothers to interpret each others' accounts, without violating confidentiality, proved important to my analysis.

Because race and ethnicity were important here, we discussed this directly. For many of the women in the sample, being in a small community with significant racial and ethnic diversity was unusual. Many of the women had never been in daily contact with members of other racial groups. As a result of this and up-close views of the other inmates brought about by shared quarters, participation in programs, and conversations with each other about families and children, inmate mothers were good observers of the class, racial, and ethnic differences between families and the implications these had for women in prison.

SUMMARY

Mothering under the best of conditions is challenging work. For inmate mothers, mothering on the inside constitutes some of hardest mothering work they will ever do. As noted in previous chapters, the resources to do mothering are not equally distributed, and these are usually at their limits when women are placed behind bars. The determination of inmate mothers to do their best to be good mothers to their children must overcome structural, economic, institutional, and other barriers to their accomplishment of that goal. The voices of the women interviewed here express the dilemmas they faced in managing motherhood in prison. With some increased attention to and advocacy for inmate mothers and for the children, caregivers, and others who are seriously affected by their incarceration, we might hope that other ways of punishment and correction can be developed and broadly implemented.

# Appendix A

# Profiles of
# Women Interviewed

*Alice:* African American woman; three children, seventeen, fifteen, and fourteen years old; not living with children before incarceration; serving three months for prostitution; thirty-nine years old; not involved with child welfare; recidivist; children with grandmother.

*April:* White woman; twelve-year-old twins; living apart from children before incarceration; twelve months for prostitution; twenty-nine years old; not involved with child welfare; recidivist; children with grandmother.

*Belinda:* African American woman; three children, one adopted, twelve, seven, and five years old; living with children prior to incarceration; serving nine months for prostitution; thirty-two years old; involved with child welfare; recidivist; one child with grandmother; two children with aunt.

*Bernice:* African American woman; two children born, five and four years old; one adopted, five years old; serving six months for prostitution; twenty-three years old; involved with child welfare; recidivist; pregnant at time of interview; child in foster care.

*Beth:* White woman; one child born and adopted, fifteen years old; not living with children prior to prison; serving six months for prostitution; thirty-four years old; involved with child welfare; recidivist; pregnant at time of interview.

*Holly:* white woman; three children, two adopted (seven-year-old twins), one nine-month-old in foster care; living apart from children before incarceration; serving eighteen months for drug delivery; thirty-seven years old; involved with child welfare; recidivist; child in foster care.

*Inez:* African American woman; six children, age twenty-one, eighteen, seventeen, twelve, eight, and five; living with children and mother prior to incarceration; serving eighteen months for drug trafficking; forty years old; not involved with child welfare; chronic recidivist; three children with grandmother; three with mother-in-law.

*Irene:* White woman; one child, eleven years old; living with children prior to incarceration; serving six years for manslaughter; twenty-nine years old; not involved with child welfare; nonrecidivist; child with grandmother.

*Kathy:* White woman; two children, seventeen and six years old; living with children prior to incarceration; serving six years for shoplifting; thirty-nine years old; not involved with child welfare; nonrecidivist; children with husband.

*Lee:* African American woman; four children, age six, four, three, and one; living with children prior to incarceration; serving a twelve-month sentence for check forgery; twenty-six years old; not involved with child welfare; nonrecidivist; children with grandmother.

*Luisa:* Hispanic woman; three children, age eleven, eight, and three; living with children before incarceration; serving six months for drug offense; thirty-five years old; not involved with child welfare; chronic recidivist; children with grandmother.

*Marcia:* White woman; one one-year-old; living with children prior to prison; serving four years for drug trafficking; thirty-four years old; not involved with child welfare; nonrecidivist; children with husband.

*Margaret:* African American woman; seven children, all adopted; not living with children prior to incarceration; serving six years for robbery; thirty-five years old; involved with child welfare; chronic recidivist.

*Maya:* African American woman; one eight-year-old child; lived with children prior to incarceration; eight-year sentence for manslaughter; thirty years old; not involved with child welfare; nonrecidivist; child with sister.

*Meredith:* White woman; two children born; one died, one fourteen-year-old living with husband; living with children before incarceration; serving twenty years for manslaughter; thirty-four years old; involved with child welfare; nonrecidivist; child with husband.

*Nicole:* White woman; two children, age six and four; living with children prior to incarceration; serving a fourteen-month sentence for forging prescriptions for drugs; twenty-six years old; not involved with child welfare; recidivist; children with grandmother.

*Paulette:* African American woman; six children, five adopted plus her two-year-old; living with her mother and with one child; serving five years for violation of probation; thirty-five years old; involved with child welfare; recidivist; child with grandmother.

*Rachel:* Hispanic woman; two children, age fifteen and thirteen; living with children before incarceration; serving twenty-year sentence for drug trafficking; thirty-four years old; not involved with child welfare; nonrecidivist; children with husband.

*Randie:* African American woman; three children, age ten, eight, and six; living with children before incarceration; serving six months for shoplifting; thirty-three years old; involved with child welfare; nonrecidivist; children with grandmother.

*Rosa:* Hispanic woman; four children, age eleven, seven, four, and three; living with children prior to incarceration; serving five years for drug trafficking; thirty-two years old; not involved with child welfare; nonrecidivist; children with grandmother

*Stacy:* White woman; one child, five years old; living with children before incarceration; serving five years for breaking and entering; twenty-two years old; involved with child welfare; recidivist; children with husband.

*Susan:* Native American woman; three children, age fifteen, thirteen, and twelve; living with children prior to prison; serving three years for fraud and assault; thirty-six years old; involved with child welfare; recidivist; children with husband.

*Tee:* African American woman; four children, age twelve, nine, seven, and six; living with children before incarceration; serving three months for fraud; thirty-two years old; involved with child welfare; recidivist; children with niece.

*Theresa:* White woman; five children, age eight, seven, two, and nine months old; one child died; living with children before incarceration; serving fifteen-year sentence for second-degree murder; twenty-five years old; involved with child welfare; nonrecidivist; children with grandmother.

*Yvonne:* Hispanic woman; three children, age eight, seven, and six months old; living with children prior to incarceration; serving eighteen months for shoplifting; thirty years old; involved with child welfare; recidivist; children with husband.

# Appendix B

| Women Interviewed* | Race/Ethnicity | Placement of Children |
|---|---|---|
| Kathy | White | Husband |
| Theresa | White | Husband |
| Holly | White | Foster care |
| Stacy | White | Husband |
| Meredith | White | Husband |
| Marcia | White | Husband |
| Beth | White | Mother |
| Nicole | White | Mother |
| April | White | Mother |
| Irene | White | Mother |
| | | |
| Susan | Native American | Husband |
| | | |
| Tee | African American | Mother/sister |
| Randie | African American | Mother |
| Alice | African American | Mother |
| Maya | African American | Sister |
| Lee | African American | Stepmother |
| Belinda | African American | Mother/aunt |
| Paulette | African American | Mother/foster |
| Inez | African American | Mother/mother-in-law |
| Bernice | African American | Foster care |
| Margaret | African American | Foster care |
| | | |
| Rachel | Hispanic | Husband |
| Yvonne | Hispanic | Husband |
| Rosa | Hispanic | Mother |
| Luisa | Hispanic | Mother |

## Others Interviewed Informally

| Lonnie | White | Foster care |
|--------|-------|-------------|
| Lucille | White | Foster care |
| Vanessa | African American | Mother/sister |
| Cynthia | African American | Mother/sister |
| Erin | African American | Foster care |
| Cathy | African American | Mother/sister |

*All names are pseudonyms.

# Bibliography

Ambert, Anne-Marie. 1994. "An International Perspective on Parenting: Social Change and Social Constructs." *Journal of Marriage and the Family* 56:529–43.

American Correctional Association. 1990. *The Female Offender: What Does the Future Hold?* Washington, D.C.: American Correctional Association.

Angel, Ronald, and Marta Tienda. 1982. "Determinants of Extended Household Structure: Cultural Pattern or Economic Need?" *American Journal of Sociology* 87:1360–83.

Arnold, Regina. 1994. "Black Women in Prison: The Price of Resistance." In *Women of Color in U.S. Society*, edited by M. Baca Zinn and B. Thorton Dill, 171–84. Philadelphia: Temple University Press.

Barry, Ellen. 1985. "Children of Prisoners: Punishing the Innocent." *Youth Law News* 6:12–17.

Baunach, Phyllis Jo. 1985. *Mothers in Prison*. New Brunswick, N.J.: Transaction Publications.

Beck, Allen J. 2000. *Prison and Jail Inmates at Midyear 1999*. Washington, D.C.: U. S. Department of Justice.

Beck, Allen J., and Darrell K. Gilliard. 1995. *Prisoners in 1994*. Washington, D.C.: U.S. Department of Justice.

Beckerman, Adela. 1991. "Women in Prison: The Conflict between Confinement and Parental Rights." *Social Justice* 18:171–83.

———. 1994. "Mothers in Prison: Meeting the Prerequisite Conditions for Permanency Planning." *Social Work* 39:9–13.

Belknap, Joanne. 1996. *The Invisible Woman: Gender, Crime, and Justice*. Belmont, Calif.: Wadsworth Publishing Company.

Billingsley, Andrew, and Jeanne H. Giovannoni. 1972. *Children of the Storm:*

*Black Children and the American Child Welfare System.* New York: Harcourt, Brace, Jovanovich.

Blinn, Cynthia. 1997. *Maternal Ties: A Selection of Programs for Female Offenders.* Washington, D.C.: American Correctional Association.

Bloom, Barbara. 1995. "Imprisoned Mothers." In *Children of Incarcerated Parents*, edited by K. Gabel and D. Johnston, 21–30. New York: Lexington Books.

Bloom, Barbara, and David Steinhart. 1993. *Why Punish the Children?: A Reappraisal of the Children of Incarcerated Mothers in America.* Washington, D.C.: National Council on Crime and Delinquency.

Boudouris, James. 1996. *Parents in Prison: Addressing the Needs of Families.* Washington, D.C.: American Correctional Association.

Bould, Sally. 1993. "Familial Caretaking: A Middle-Range Definition of Family in the Context of Social Policy." *Journal of Family Issues* 14:133–51.

Breakwell, Glynis M. 1986. *Coping with Threatened Identities.* New York: Methuen.

Bresler, Laura, and Diane K. Lewis. 1986. "Black and White Women Prisoners: Differences in Family Ties and Their Programmatic Implications." *The Prison Journal* 63:116–22.

Burton, Linda M. 1992. "Black Grandparents Rearing Children of Drug-Addicted Parents: Stressors, Outcomes, and Social Service Needs." *The Gerontologist* 32:744–51.

Burton, Linda M., and Carol B. Stack. 1992. "Conscripting Kin: Reflections on Family, Generation, and Culture." In *Family, Self, and Society: Toward a New Agenda for Family Research*, edited by P. A. Cowan et al., 103–13. Hillsdale, N.J.: Lawrence Erlbaum Associates.

Butterfield, Fox. 1999. "As Inmate Population Grows, So Does a Focus on Children." *New York Times*, 7 April.

Caplan, Paula J., and Ian Hall-McCorquodale. 1985. "Mother-blaming in Major Clinical Journals." *American Journal of Orthopsychiatry* 55:345–53.

Charmaz, Kathy. 1983. "The Grounded Theory Method: An Explication and Interpretation." In *Contemporary Field Research: A Collection of Readings*, edited by R. M. Emerson, 109–26. Boston: Little, Brown.

Cheal, David. 1991. *Family and the State of Theory.* Toronto, Ont.: University of Toronto Press.

Chesney-Lind, Meda. 1993. "Sentencing Women to Prison: Equality without Justice." Presented at the Seventh National Roundtable on Women in Prison, 20 June, Washington, D.C.

———. 1997. *The Female Offender: Girls, Women, and Crime.* Thousand Oaks, Calif.: Sage Publications.

Chesney-Lind, Meda, and Russ Immarigeon. 1995. "Alternatives to Women's Incarceration ." In *Children of Incarcerated Parents*, edited by K. Gabel and D. Johnston, 299–309. New York: Lexington Books.

Coffey, Amanda, and Paul Atkinson. 1996. *Making Sense of Qualitative Data: Complementary Research Strategies*. Thousand Oaks, Calif.: Sage Publications.

Collins, Patricia Hill. 1990. *Black Feminist Thought: Knowledge, Consciousness, and the Politics of Empowerment*. New York: Routledge.

———. 1994. "Shifting the Center: Race, Class, and Feminist Theorizing about Motherhood." In *Mothering: Ideology, Experience, and Agency*, edited by E. N. Glenn, G. Chang, and L. R. Forcey, 45–66. New York: Routledge.

Daly, Kathleen. 1987. "Discrimination in the Criminal Courts: Family, Gender, and the Problem of Equal Treatment." *Social Forces* 66:152–75.

———. 1994. *Gender, Crime, and Punishment*. New Haven: Yale University Press.

Daly, Kathleen, and Meda Chesney-Lind. 1988. "Feminism and Criminology." *Justice Quarterly* 5:497–535.

Day, Randall D., and Wade C. Mackey. 1988. "Children as Resources: A Cultural Approach." *Family Perspective* 20:251–64.

Denzin, Norman K. 1989. *The Research Act: A Theoretical Introduction to Sociological Methods*. 3d ed. Englewood Cliffs, N.J.: Prentice-Hall

DeVault, Marjorie. 1991. *Feeding the Family: The Social Organization of Caring as Gendered Work*. Chicago: University of Chicago Press.

———. 1995. "Ethnicity and Expertise: Racial-Ethnic Knowledge in Sociological Research." *Gender and Society* 9:612–31.

DiMascio, William M. 1997. *Seeking Justice: Crime and Punishment in America*. New York: The Edna McConnell Clark Foundation.

Donzelot, Jacques. 1979. *The Policing of Families*. New York: Pantheon.

Donziger, Stephen R. 1996. *The Real War on Crime: The Report of the National Criminal Justice Commission*. New York: HarperPerennial.

Dressel, Paula L., and Sandra K. Barnhill. 1994. "Reframing Gerontological Thought and Practice: The Case of Grandmothers with Daughters in Prison." *The Gerontologist* 34:685–91.

Ehrenreich, Barbara, and Deirdre English. 1978. *For Her Own Good: 150 Years of the Experts' Advice to Women*. New York: Anchor Books.

Farber, Bernard. 1964. *Family: Organization and Interaction*. San Francisco: Chandler Publishing Company.

Farrell, Ann. 1998. "Mothers Offending against Their Role: An Australian Experience." *Women and Criminal Justice* 9, no. 4:47–67.

Fessler, Susan Rakovitz. 1991. "Mothers in the Correctional System: Separation from Children and Reunification after Incarceration." Ph.D. dissertation, State University of New York at Albany.

Finch, Janet. 1989. *Family Obligations and Social Change*. Cambridge, England: Polity Press.

Fine, Michelle. 1998. "Working the Hyphens: Reinventing Self and Other in Qualitative Research." In *The Landscape of Qualitative Research: Theories and Issues*, edited by N. K. Denzin and Y. S. Lincoln, 130–53. Thousand Oaks, Calif.: Sage Publications.

Garey, Anita Ita. 1995. "Constructing Motherhood on the Night Shift: 'Working Mothers' as 'Stay-at-Home Moms'." *Qualitative Sociology* 18:415–37.

Gaudin, James M., and Richard Sutphen. 1993. "Foster Care vs. Extended Family Care for Children of Incarcerated Mothers." *Journal of Offender Rehabilitation* 19:129–47.

Genty, Philip M. 1995. "Termination of Parental Rights among Prisoners." In *Children of Incarcerated Parents*, edited by K. Gabel and D. Johnston, 167–82. New York: Lexington Books.

Gilliard, Darrell K. 1999. *Prison and Jail Inmates at Midyear 1998*. Washington, D.C.: U.S. Department of Justice.

Glenn, Evelyn Nakano. 1987. "Gender and the Family." In *Analyzing Gender: A Handbook of Social Science Research*, edited by B. B. Hess and M. M. Ferree, 348–80. Newbury Park, Calif.: Sage Publications.

———. 1994. "Social Constructions of Mothering: A Thematic View." In *Mothering: Ideology, Experience, and Agency*, edited by E. N. Glenn, G. Chang, and L. R. Forcey, 1–32. New York: Routledge.

Glick, Ruth M., and Virginia V. Neto. 1977. *National Study of Women's Correctional Programs*. Washington, D.C.: U. S. Department of Justice.

Goffman, Erving. 1959. *The Presentation of Self in Everyday Life*. New York: Doubleday.

———. 1961. *Asylums: Essays on the Social Situation of Mental Patients and Other Inmates*. Garden City, N.Y.: Anchor Books.

———. 1963. *Stigma: Notes on the Management of Spoiled Identity*. Englewood Cliffs, N.J.: Prentice-Hall.

Golden, Renny. 1997. *Disposable Children: America's Welfare System*. Belmont, Calif.: Wadsworth Publishing.

Goode, William. 1964. *The Family*. Englewood Cliffs, N.J.: Prentice-Hall.

Gordon, Linda. 1988. *Heroes of Their Own Lives: The Politics and History of Family Violence*. New York: Viking Press.

Griffith, Allison, and Dorothy E. Smith. 1987. "Constructing Cultural Knowledge: Mothering as Discourse." In *Women and Education: A Canadian Perspective*, edited by J. Gaskell and A. McLaren, 87–103. Calgary, Alta.: Detselig.

Gubrium, Jaber F., and James A. Holstein. 1990. *What is Family?* Mountain View, Calif.: Mayfield Publishing Company.

Hairston, Creasie Finney. 1991. "Mothers in Jail: Parent-Child Separation and Jail Visitation." *Affilia* 6:9–27.

Haley, Kathleen. 1977. "Mothers behind Bars: A Look at the Parental Rights of Incarcerated Women." *New England Journal on Prison Law* 4:141–55.

Hammersley, Martyn. 1990. *Reading Ethnographic Research: A Critical Guide.* London: Longman.

Harlow, Caroline Wolf. 1999. *Prior Abuse Reported by Inmates and Probationers.* Washington, D.C.: U.S. Department of Justice.

Hays, Sharon. 1996. *The Cultural Contradictions of Motherhood.* New Haven: Yale University Press.

Heidensohn, Frances. 1987. "Women and Crime: Questions for Criminology." In *Gender, Crime and Justice*, edited by P. Carlen and A. Worrall, 16–28. London: Open University Press.

———. 1995. *Women and Crime.* 2d ed. New York: New York University Press.

Henriques, Zelma Weston. 1982. *Imprisoned Mothers and Their Children: A Descriptive and Analytical Study.* Washington, D.C.: University Press of America.

Hill, Reuben. 1949. *Families under Stress.* New York: Harper and Row.

Hirschi, Travis. 1969. *Causes of Delinquency.* Berkeley: University of California Press.

Hungerford, Gregory. 1996. "Caregivers of Children Whose Mothers Are Incarcerated." *Children Today* 24:23–27.

Hunter, Susan M. 1984. "The Relationship between Women Offenders and Their Children." Ph. D. dissertation, Michigan State University.

Immarigeon, Russ. 1995. "Correctional Options: What Works?" *Corrections Today* 57: insert.

Johnston, Denise. 1995a. "The Care and Placement of Prisoners' Children." In *Children of Incarcerated Parents*, edited by K. Gabel and D. Johnston, 103–23. New York: Lexington Books.

———. 1995b. "Child Custody Issues of Women Prisoners: A Preliminary Report from the CHICAS Project." *The Prison Journal* 75:222–39.

———. 1995c. "The Effects of Parental Incarceration." In *Children of Incarcerated Parents*, edited by K. Gabel and D. Johnston, 59–88. New York: Lexington Books.

Kampfner, Christina Jose. 1995. "Post-Traumatic Stress Reactions in Children of Incarcerated Mothers." In *Children of Incarcerated Parents*, edited by K. Gabel and D. Johnston, 89–100. New York: Lexington Books.

Katz, Jack. 1983. "A Theory of Qualitative Methodology: The Social System of Analytic Fieldwork." In *Contemporary Field Research: A Collection of Readings*, edited by R. M. Emerson, 127–48. Prospect Heights, Ill.: Waveland Press.

Kearney, Margaret H., and Sheigla Murphy. 1993. *At Least I Feel Guilty: Emotions and Reflexivity in Pregnant Drug Users' Accounts*. San Francisco: Institute for Scientific Analysis.

Kiser, George. 1991. "Female Inmates and Their Families." *Federal Probation*, September, 56–63.

Koban, Linda A. 1985. "Parents in Prison: A Comparitive Analysis of the Effects of Incarceration on the Families of Men and Women." *Research in Law, Deviance, and Social Control* 5:171–83.

Kruttschnitt, Candace. 1981. "Social Status and the Sentencing of Female Offenders." *Law and Society Review* 15:247–65.

Leach, Penelope. 1988. *Baby and Child: From Birth to Age Five*. Harmondsworth, U.K.: Penguin.

LeFlore, Larry, and Mary Ann Holston. 1989. "Perceived Importance of Parenting Behaviors as Reported by Inmate Mothers: An Exploratory Study." *Journal of Offender Counseling, Services and Rehabilitation* 14:5–21.

Leonard, Eileen B. 1982. *Women, Crime, and Society: A Critique of Theoretical Criminology*. London: Longman.

Lincoln, Yvonna S., and Egon C. Guba. 1985. *Naturalistic Inquiry*. Beverly Hills, Calif.: Sage Publications.

Lowenstein, A. 1986. "Temporary Single Parenthood: The Case of Prisoners' Families." *Family Relations* 36:79–85.

Maguire, Kathleen, and Ann L. Pastore, eds. 1998. *Sourcebook of Criminal Justice Statistics, 1997*. U.S. Department of Justice, Bureau of Justice Statistics. Washington, D.C.: Government Printing Office.

Mahan, Sue. 1982. *Unfit Mothers*. Palo Alto, Calif.: R&E Research Associates.

Maher, Lisa. 1992. "Punishment and Welfare: Crack Cocaine and the Regulation of Mothering." In *The Criminalization of a Woman's Body*, edited by C. Feinman, 157–92. New York: Harrington Park Press.

Marshall, Harriette. 1991. "The Social Construction of Motherhood: An Analysis of Childcare and Parenting Manuals." In *Motherhood: Meanings, Practices, and Ideologies*, edited by A. Phoenix, A. Woollett, and E. Lloyd, 66–85. New York: Sage Publications.

Martin, Elmer P., and Joanne M. Martin. 1978. *The Black Extended Family.* Chicago: University of Chicago Press.

Martin, Mary. 1997. "Connected Mothers: A Follow-Up Study of Incarcerated Women and Their Children." *Women and Criminal Justice* 8, no. 4:1–23.

Mauer, Mark. 1997. "Americans behind Bars: U.S. and International Use of Incarceration, 1995." Washington, D.C.: The Sentencing Project.

McDonald, Cameron L. 1998. "Manufacturing Motherhood: The Shadow Work of Nannies and Au Pairs." *Qualitative Sociology* 21:25–53.

McGowan, Brenda G., and Karen L. Blumenthal. 1978. *Why Punish the Children?* Hackensack, N.J.: National Council on Crime and Delinquency.

McMahon, Martha. 1995. *Engendering Motherhood: Identity and Self-Transformation in Women's Lives.* New York: Guilford Press.

Miller, Eleanor M. 1986. *Street Woman.* Philadelphia: Temple University Press.

———. 1988. "'Some Peoples Calls It Crime': Hustling, the Illegal Work of Underclass Women." In *The Worth of Women's Work: A Qualitative Synthesis,* edited by A. Strathan, E. Miller, and H. Mausch, 109–32. Albany: State University of New York Press.

Nelson, Margaret K. 1994. "Family Day Care Providers: Dilemmas of Daily Practice." In *Mothering: Ideology, Experience, and Agency,* edited by E. N. Glenn, G. Chang, and L. R. Forcey, 181–209. New York: Routledge.

Neto, Virginia V., and LaNelle Marie Bainer. 1983. "Mother and Wife Locked Up: A Day with the Family." *The Prison Journal* 63:124–41.

Oakley, Ann. 1976. *Woman's Work: The Housewife, Past and Present.* New York: Pantheon Books.

Owen, Barbara, and Barbara Bloom. 1995. "Profiling Women Prisoners." *The Prison Journal* 75:165–85.

Parsons, Talcott. 1964. *The Social System.* New York: Free Press.

Peterson, Jean Trellogen. 1993. "Generalized Extended Family Exchange: A Case from the Philippines." *Journal of Marriage and the Family* 55:57–84.

Phoenix, Ann, and Anne Woollett. 1991. "Motherhood: Social Constructions, Politics, and Psychology." In *Motherhood: Meanings, Practices, and Ideologies,* edited by A. Phoenix, A. Woollett, and E. Lloyd, 13–27. New York: Sage Publications.

Raeder, Myrna S. 1993. "Gender and Sentencing: Single Moms, Battered Women, and Other Sex-Based Anomalies in the Gender-Free World of the Federal Sentencing Guidelines." *Pepperdine Law Review* 20:905–90.

Rafter, Nicole Hahn. 1997. *Partial Justice: Women, Prisons, and Social Control.* 2d ed. New Brunswick, N.J.: Transaction.

Raley, R. Kelly. 1995. "Black-White Differences in Kin Contact and Exchange among Never Married Adults." *Journal of Family Issues* 16:77–103.

Rhode Island Department of Corrections. 1996. *Semi-Annual Population Report: July–December 1996.* Cranston, R.I.

———. 1997. *Statistical Report —Women's Facilities.* Cranston, R.I.

Richie, Beth E. 1996. *Compelled to Crime: The Gender Entrapment of Battered Black Women.* New York: Routledge.

Roschelle, Anne R. 1997. *No More Kin: Exploring Race, Class, and Gender in Family Networks.* Thousand Oaks, Calif.: Sage Publications.

Rosenbaum, Jill Leslie, and James Lasley. 1990. "School, Community Context, and Delinquency." *Justice Quarterly* 7:493–513.

Rothman, Barbara Katz. 1987. *The Tentative Pregnancy: Prenatal Diagnosis and the Future of Motherhood.* New York: Penguin Books.

Schatzman, Leonard. 1991. "Dimensional Analysis: Notes on an Alternative Approach to the Grounding of Theory in Qualitative Research." In *Social Organization and Social Process: Essays in Honor of Anselm Strauss,* edited by D. R. Maines, 303–14. New York: Aldine de Gruyter.

Schur, Edwin M. 1983. *Labeling Women Deviant: Gender, Stigma, and Social Control.* Philadelphia: Temple University Press.

Showers, Jacy. 1993. "Assessing and Remedying Parenting Knowledge among Women Inmates." *Journal of Offender Rehabilitation* 20:35–46.

Smart, Carol. 1976. *Women, Crime, and Criminology: A Feminist Critique.* London: Routledge.

———. 1996. "Deconstructing Motherhood." In *Good Enough Mothering?,* edited by E. Bortolaia, 37–57. London: Routledge.

Smith, Dorothy E. 1993. "The Standard North American Family: SNAF as an Ideological Code." *Signs* 14:50–65.

Snell, Tracy L. 1994. *Women in Prison: Survey of State Prison Inmates, 1991.* Washington, D.C.: U.S. Department of Justice.

Snow, David A., and Leon Anderson. 1987. "Identity Work among the Homeless: The Verbal Construction and Avowal of Personal Identities." *American Journal of Sociology* 92:1336–71.

———. 1993. *Down on Their Luck: A Study of Homeless Street People.* Berkeley: University of California Press.

Solinger, Ricki. 1992. *Wake Up Little Susie: Single Pregnancy and Race before Roe v. Wade.* London: Routledge.

Spock, Benjamin. 1988. *Dr. Spock's Baby and Child Care.* 40th Anniversary ed. London: Allen.

Stacey, Judith. 1990. *Brave New Families: Stories of Domestic Upheaval in Late-Twentieth-Century America*. New York: Basic Books.

Stack, Carol B. 1974. *All Our Kin: Strategies for Survival in a Black Community*. New York: Harper and Row.

Stanton, Ann M. 1980. *When Mothers Go to Jail*. Lexington, Mass.: D. C. Heath and Company.

Strauss, Anselm, and Juliet Corbin. 1990. *Basics of Qualitative Research: Grounded Theory Procedures and Techniques*. Newbury Park, Calif.: Sage Publications.

Stuart, Reginald. 1997. "Behind Bars: The Growing Number of Black Women in Prison Saps Families and Meager Community Resources." *Emerge*, March, 44–48.

Swan, L. Alex. 1981. *Families of Black Prisoners: Survival and Progress*. Boston: G. K. Hall and Co.

Sykes, Gresham. 1958. *The Society of Captives*. Princeton: Princeton University Press.

Tajfel, Henri. 1978. *Differentiation between Social Groups: Studies in the Social Psychology of Intergroup Relations*. London: Academic Press.

Taylor, Jill McLean, Carol Gilligan, and Amy M. Sullivan. 1995. *Between Voice and Silence: Women and Girls, Race and Relationship*. Cambridge: Harvard University Press.

Taylor, Robert Joseph. 1986. "Receipt of Support from Family among Black Americans: Demographic and Family Differences." *Journal of Marriage and the Family* 48:67–77.

Thornburg, Tracy, and Diane Trunk. 1992. "A Collage of Voices: A Dialogue with Women in Prison." *Southern California Review of Law and Women's Studies* 2:155–217.

Thorne, Barrie. 1992. "Feminism and the Family: Two Decades of Thought." In *Rethinking the Family: Two Decades of Thought*, edited by B. Thorne and M. Yalom, 1–30. 2d ed. Boston: Northeastern University Press.

Thurer, Shari L. 1994. *The Myths of Motherhood: How Culture Reinvents the Good Mother*. Boston: Houghton Mifflin.

Toby, Jackson. 1957. "Social Disorganization and Stake in Conformity: Complementary Factors in the Predatory Behaviors of Hoodlums." *Journal of Criminal Law, Criminology, and Police Science* 48:12–17.

Uttal, Lynet. 1994. "Good Mothers, Bad Mothers, Other Mothers: Making Sense of Child Care." Memphis, Tenn.: Center for Research on Women.

Washington, Valora. 1988. "The Black Mother in the United States: History, Theory, Research, and Issues." In *The Different Faces of Motherhood*, edited by B. Birns and D. F. Hay, 185–213. New York: Plenum Press.

Zalba, Serapio R. 1964. "Inmate-Mothers and Their Children." In *Deviancy and the Family*, edited by C. D. Bryant and J. G. Wells, 181–89. Philadelphia: F. A. Davis Company.

Zelizer, Viviana A. 1985. *Pricing the Priceless Child*. New York: Basic Books.

Zinn, Maxine Baca. 1994. "Feminist Rethinking from Racial-Ethnic Families." In *Women of Color in U.S. Society*, edited by M. B. Zinn and B. T. Dill, 303–14. Philadelphia: Temple University Press.

# Index

173